Weddingology

Second Edition

Weddingology

A Wedding Encyclopedia

Second Edition

Shari Grenier

iUniverse®

WEDDINGOLOGY
A WEDDING ENCYCLOPEDIA

iUniverse books may be ordered through booksellers or by contacting:

iUniverse
1663 Liberty Drive
Bloomington, IN 47403
www.iuniverse.com
1-800-Authors (1-800-288-4677)

ISBN: 978-1-5320-4921-7 (sc)
ISBN: 978-1-5320-4922-4 (e)

Library of Congress Control Number: 2018905454

Print information available on the last page.

iUniverse rev. date: 05/15/2018

ALSO BY SHARI GRENIER

The Sandcastles Guide to Starting and Managing Your Own Wedding-Planning Business

The Proverbs Principle

This book is dedicated to my husband, Dave Grenier, with beautiful memories of our storybook wedding.

Contents

About the Author

Shari Grenier is a graduate of the University of Waterloo (Religious Studies) and the New York School of Interior Design.

As the head of *Interior Motives*, Shari enjoyed a successful career in the design field, including developing and teaching an interior decorating course for a local college. She opened *Sandcastles* in 1996, to use her flair with color, fabrics and space planning in the field of wedding consulting. Since then, Shari has helped countless brides plan their dream weddings, and certified many wedding planners.

Most recently, Shari's business interests are centered around Proverbs 31 Lifestyles. As the tagline of the business indicates, it covers "your wedding, your faith, your home, your life."

On any given day, Shari can be found helping a client organize their closets, meeting a newly engaged couple to help plan their wedding, leading a Bible study group, certifying wedding planners, or staging a home for sale.

Shari's other books include *The Proverbs Principle* and *The Sandcastles Guide to Starting and Managing Your Own Wedding-Planning Business.*

Acknowledgment

The cover photograph is used with the kind permission of
Laura and Davin MacKinnon

Introduction

You're getting married! Never again will you be making so many choices, spending so much money, or planning such a lavish party! Don't you wish you could do it all with the skill of a professional wedding planner?

Now you can!

As one of the textbooks for *The Sandcastles Wedding Consultant Certification Programme*, this book is used to teach wedding planners how to plan beautiful weddings. Over and over, students have told me, "I wish there had been a book like this when I was planning my own wedding."

Now there is!

Weddingology will take you step-by-step through the process of planning your wedding, using the same methods our students learn in order to become certified wedding planners.

Anyone who has ever planned their wedding will tell you that it's a lot of hard work and it can be very stressful at times. But they will also tell you that nothing can compare with the feeling you get when it's all over and you're sitting with your new husband, looking at your wedding pictures.

From your engagement to your honeymoon, and even setting up your first home, *Weddingology* will help you make your dream wedding a reality!

CHAPTER 1

Early Planning

The length of an engagement is usually a matter of convenience. Many engaged couples set a wedding date soon after the engagement is announced; others plan a longer engagement.

Both sets of parents *must* be told of the engagement before anyone else. Once your parents have been told of the engagement, you can start telling all your friends. You may also place a notice in your local newspaper. If this is to be a long engagement, wait until the wedding is a couple of months away.

Nowadays, the engaged couple places the announcement themselves, although the parents occasionally do it. If the parents are divorced, the mother makes the announcement of her child's engagement.

The announcement will run in the newspaper of the city or town in which you live. If your parents live elsewhere, it may also run in their local paper. If there has recently been a death in the immediate family, it is not considered proper to place a notice in the newspaper; word-of-mouth announcements are acceptable.

The announcement gives the full names of the bride and groom, the names of their parents, details of the upcoming wedding, the location of the honeymoon, and the intended residence after the wedding. A photograph is optional. If a parent is deceased, the word "late" will precede their name. Provide a telephone number where you can be reached for verification. If you plan to make a surprise announcement at the engagement party, specify a release date with your submission. That way, no one will read about it in the papers first.

The Engagement Party

The happy news can be celebrated with an engagement party. Often, the engagement is not announced until the guests have assembled.

Traditionally, the engagement party is hosted by the bride's parents, often at home. Depending upon the size of the guest list, however, it may be necessary to rent a venue.

As a rule, the formality of the engagement party is an indication of the formality of the wedding to follow. It can be anything from a formal sit-down dinner, to an afternoon tea, to a backyard barbecue.

The formality of the invitations is in keeping with the formality of the party. Handwritten invitations are proper for an informal party. The wording will depend upon whether guests already know of the engagement or if it is intended to be a surprise. Regardless, guests are still expected to RSVP.

Gifts are not mandatory, but many guests will bring one. Thank-you notes must be sent out promptly.

As for the festivities themselves, just relax and have fun. The only set protocol is that the father of the bride proposes a toast to the couple.

Buying a Diamond

Many couples shop together for the bride's engagement ring, but some lucky girls are still surprised by a proposal and a ring just when they least expect it!

Buy the diamond from a reputable source. Large jewelry stores are more likely to offer sale prices, but small independent jewelers will often custom-design the ring for you. It is important that the jeweler have the proper credentials. The Canadian Institute of Gemology and The Gemological Institute of America certify jewelers with the designation "Accredited Gemologist."

Diamonds are identified and graded according to the 4 C's–Cut, Carat, Clarity, and Color.

A carat is one-fifth of a gram, or two hundred milligrams. Diamonds are weighed in points. One hundred points equal one carat. Therefore, you can easily tell the weight of a stone. For example, a quarter-carat diamond is twenty-five points. If the ring has more than one diamond, it will wear a tag stating the TCW or Total Carat Weight. A diamond just under a carat will be priced considerably less than a full carat, yet the difference in size will not be noticeable. Sample diameters of various-sized diamonds are as follows:

- .25 carat: 4 mm
- .50 carat: 5 mm
- .75 carat: 6 mm
- 1 carat: 6.5 mm

Clarity refers to the presence or absence of small black flecks in a diamond. These are caused by carbon, and are sometimes called "beauty marks." Larger ones can be easily seen. Often it takes a jeweler's loupe, which magnifies the diamond ten times, to see them. A good way to get a larger stone for the same money is to buy one that has defects not visible to the naked eye. Diamonds are rated on a scale of F1 (flawless) to I3 (imperfect).

The color of a diamond helps determine its value. A true white diamond is rare; most have a small amount of color. Colored diamonds are called "fancies," and come in pink, yellow, blue, and even black. Diamonds are rated on a scale of D (colorless) to Z.

The cut is what gives a diamond its fire. The best-cut diamonds are those into which light enters, disperses, and reflects back to the eye.

Diamonds come in many shapes. The best known of these is the round brilliant, which is also the most expensive. Others are pear, heart, emerald (rectangular), oval, princess (square), and marquise (pointed on both ends).

If a diamond ring is over one carat, it should be accompanied by an appraisal. This will record the value of the ring, the size, cut, clarity, and color of the stone, and a description of the setting. In addition, it maps the diamond, showing each of the carbon marks, its size, and its location. The appraisal is not to be confused with a diamond certificate, which is issued on loose stones only.

Wedding Rings

Until the Second World War, few grooms wore wedding rings. But soldiers marrying and leaving to go overseas wanted something tangible to take with them; the double-ring ceremony became more common. Many couples follow the custom of engraving the inside of the band with the date and their initials.

Wedding bands and engagement rings are often bought as a set. Yellow gold is the most popular, followed by white gold, rose gold, and platinum. White and yellow gold are often used together. Many designs are set with diamonds. Some Orthodox and Jewish ceremonies do not allow ornamentation. If the bride wants a more decorative ring than a plain gold band, her fiancé can have one blessed and give it to her as a wedding gift.

The engagement ring is moved to the right hand for the ceremony and switched back before the reception.

What is Your Bridal Personality?

Before you can plan your perfect wedding, you must determine your personal style. It will shine through everywhere on your wedding day, so don't try to be someone you're not.

Traditional: You like timeless looks and understated elegance. When planning your wedding, you will follow the etiquette books to the letter.

Romantic: You want your wedding to be straight out of a Jane Austen novel. You love bows, flowers, embroidery, lace–all the trimmings.

Dramatic: You love the glamour of Hollywood, and you have what it takes to pull it off. Red roses, slinky gowns, and diamonds give you the look you want.

Free Spirit: You prefer wildflowers to red roses. Your gown will be comfortable and flow freely. You wish you could get married in bare feet!

Sophisticated: You feel at home in Paris and New York. You can spot a Chanel a mile away. "Exquisite" is the word that comes to mind when describing your wedding.

Modern: You believe that "less is more," and your wedding shows it. You may not be a minimalist, but you certainly like to keep things simple. Ornamentation and excessive decoration is not for you.

Girl Next Door: You are not interested in outdoing anyone. You are comfortable just being yourself. You may want to wear your mother's pearls on your wedding day.

Degree of Formality

It is important to determine the formality of the wedding from the start, as this will affect many other details.

Ultra-formal: The ultra-formal wedding is always held in a church, unless a wealthy family has an estate befitting such a wedding. The bride's gown has a long train, and there are between six and twelve bridesmaids. If the wedding is to be held in the Catholic Church, it will take place with Mass before noon. Otherwise, it will be held at noon or late afternoon. This type of wedding is always followed by a lavish sit-down reception.

Formal: The formal wedding takes place at noon or later in the afternoon, unless it is a Catholic wedding. In that case, it will take place with Mass before noon. This wedding is most often held in a church, although it can also be held at home, in a hotel ballroom, at a historical location, or in a garden. There are about six bridesmaids and groomsmen, in equal numbers. The ceremony is followed by a reception.

Semiformal: The semiformal wedding is held in a church, chapel, hotel, garden, or home. The ceremony is held in the morning for a Catholic wedding, and any time of the day for other ceremonies. There are fewer than six bridesmaids and groomsmen. It is followed by a reception.

Informal: The informal wedding can be held at any location, often in the church rectory. There are no formal attendants, but two special friends are chosen to stand up for the couple. Dress is simple, as are decorations. There is usually no processional. The reception following is often a buffet.

Determining Priorities

It is impossible for any bride to take all of her dreams and ideas for the perfect wedding and put them together–that would take several weddings! You must determine your priorities.

Remember that this wedding is the beginning of your life together. Although you want to accommodate your families and others you love, they are not the ones for whom this wedding must have the most meaning. Decide what is the most important to *you*, and then remain firm. Anything else will represent an area in which you can comprise.

You still have the final say in all decisions. Usually, these decisions translate into dollars. For instance, which do you prefer?

- Large or small wedding?
- Formal or informal?
- Sit-down dinner or cocktail reception?
- Band or DJ?

Jot down everything you want and place a dollar figure beside each. On a second list, include anything that is important to your families; again, include a dollar figure.

The budget will include every item on the first list, but it may not be financially possible to include all of the items on the second list. In this case, number each item in order of priority. This will ensure that the most important items will be taken care of.

The Language of Color

When you choose a color scheme for your wedding, chances are you will build it around your favorite color. Traditionally, colors have associations. If you can't decide, consider one with a relevant meaning:

Red or Fuchsia: In India or China, the color of love

Green: Ancient color of fertility and the lucky color of the Italians and the Irish

Red and Yellow: The marriage colors of Egypt, Russia, and the Orient

Blue or Turquoise: The color of loyalty; made popular by "something old, something new, something borrowed, something blue"

Purple: Classic color of royalty; ancient Greek color of wealth

Blue and Gold: Power, dignity, and wealth

Contracts With Vendors

Contracts spell out your legal rights and obligations, as well as those of the vendors. They are legally binding documents, so have the contract checked over by your wedding planner or a trusted family member before you sign anything. The contract must include the following:

- Parties to the contract (you, your fiancé, and the vendor)
- Services to be provided, in specific detail
- Time period in which the services are to be provided
- The person who is to provide the services
- Total fee, including all service charges and taxes
- Amount of deposit and the date due
- Payments due before the wedding date, and the due dates for each
- Amount of the final payment, and the due date
- Cancellation policies
- Provision for changes
- Any disclaimers

Deposits are usually due when the contract is signed, and final payment is due in the days leading up to the wedding. Many vendors will not accommodate a change in the wedding date and any such change will involve a new contract, a new deposit, and the forfeiture of any payments made to date. Most contracts require changes to be made in writing and signed by all parties.

The photographer, videographer, wedding planner, and any other person who is working the entire day and evening should be included in the head count for meals. Ask your caterer to provide a less expensive meal for your vendors.

Tipping Vendors

Tips are given as a personal expression of gratitude. Gratuities are almost always added into the final bill. If a particular server has spent the evening providing you with service over and above your expectations, you may wish to give that individual a tip; the customary amount would be up to fifteen percent. Others falling into this category include catering managers, hotel banquet managers, waiters, waitresses, bartenders, and wedding planners. Others can be tipped as follows:

Coatroom attendants: Fifty cents to one dollar per guest; it may be to your advantage to arrange for a flat fee prior to the wedding.

Limousine driver: Fifteen to twenty percent; be sure to read your contract, as often the tip has already been added to the final bill.

Florist, photographer, baker, and musicians: Up to fifteen percent; tip for extra services only.

Civil ceremony officiant: (Judge, Justice of the Peace, City Clerk): Between fifty dollars and seventy-five dollars; if travel is involved, an additional gratuity is expected.

Clergy, rabbi, or priest: It is normal to give one hundred dollars; if travel is involved, an additional gratuity is appreciated.

Organist: Fifty dollars is appropriate unless the organist is a family member or close friend.

The Wedding Budget

Rare is the wedding with an unlimited budget, and some weddings have very tight restrictions. Instead of worrying about the amount that you can spend, take the budget and work with it to get the most for your money.

Every wedding, no matter how large or small, must have a written budget. This way, you and your fiancé can work together to determine your priorities and explore ideas to stretch your wedding dollars.

Compromise is the best way to get the wedding of your dreams within your budget. A certain flower may have to be substituted with a less expensive one in season. If you have your heart set on a particular flower for your bouquet, the altar decorations can be of a less expensive flower.

Friends may offer to provide the transportation, handle hair and makeup for the wedding party, or videotape the wedding. However, unless the friend is a professional photographer, it is not wise to accept the offer of free wedding pictures, as so much can affect the quality of the finished photos.

Wedding venues are subject to peak seasons; other times of the year may be less expensive. The same is true of weekdays and Sundays. Remember, though, that even a weekday or Sunday wedding during the busy season could cost more than a Saturday wedding during the low period.

You can find bargains on wedding gowns if you are willing to shop "off the rack." Samples and discontinued gowns are often sold at a deep discount. Never be discouraged if you see a gown in a magazine that turns out to be too expensive. It may be possible to find a similar gown that is less costly, perhaps in a different fabric or by a different manufacturer.

Many wedding receptions feature cocktails and hors d'oeuvres instead of the traditional buffet or sit-down dinner. An afternoon tea reception with small sandwiches and champagne is also charming and affordable.

Potted plants can be taken from the ceremony to the reception to help you cut decorating costs. Many florists will rent these to you.

Elegance is the least expensive way to go because a little goes a long way, and a little of a good thing often costs less than you think!

Who Pays For What?

The following list breaks down the traditional wedding expenses according to who is responsible for them. Even these days, some parents pay for their daughter's wedding with all the trimmings. However, couples are marrying later and often pay for their own weddings, so it is no longer considered a parent's obligation.

Traditionally, the bride's parents paid for the wedding and reception. If the bride's parents were divorced, the bride's father paid for the entire wedding.

The groom's parents traditionally handled the costs of the reception dinner, as well as the corsages and boutonnieres for the parents and grandparents on both sides. These days, they take a larger financial responsibility, often hosting the bar or paying for a portion of the reception.

Bride's Family

- Engagement party
- Bride's attire and trousseau
- Ceremony site rental, organist, and soloist
- Extras for ceremony, such as aisle runner or candelabra
- Wedding party's transportation to the ceremony and reception
- Flowers for the bridesmaids, maid of honor, and flower girl
- Ceremony and reception flowers
- Reception costs
- Photography
- Their wedding gift to the couple

The Bride

- Groom's wedding ring
- Her wedding gift to the groom
- Her gifts to her attendants
- Wedding accessories, such as guest book, plume pen, cake knife, etc.
- Her hair, makeup, and nails
- Thank-you notes, personal stationery

- Wedding planner
- Lunch with bridesmaids

The Groom's Family

- Boutonnieres for fathers and grandfathers (sometimes paid for by the groom)
- Corsages for mothers and grandmothers (sometimes paid for by the groom)
- Rehearsal dinner
- Their attire
- Their gift to the couple
- Their travel and accommodation
- Any other wedding costs they wish to offer; the groom's family often covers the cost of the bar

The Groom

- Bride's engagement and wedding rings
- His gift to the bride
- His gifts to his attendants
- Marriage license
- Officiant's fee
- Bride's bouquet
- Boutonnieres for himself and his attendants

Attendants (or Parents of Child Attendants)

- Their gifts to the couple (or a joint gift)
- Their attire (rental or purchase)
- Travel expenses

Weekend Weddings

Many families find themselves scattered from one end of the country to the other. When they gather for a family wedding, it turns into a family reunion. Hence, the "weekend wedding" was born.

Beginning on the Friday, the rehearsal dinner can be expanded to include everyone. It can take the form of a barbecue or pizza party if there will be too many people for a more traditional rehearsal dinner.

Saturday is the day of the wedding. Depending on the time of the ceremony, the guests attend a large breakfast or brunch, which leads up to the ceremony and reception. The bride and groom, their parents, and the wedding party are very busy at this time, and are not expected to attend.

Sunday, the day after the wedding, is a good day to sleep in and perhaps do some sightseeing. Guests can enjoy a game of golf or relax around the swimming pool. Later, they depart for home, saying good-bye to the bride and groom, who will leave for their honeymoon.

Weekend weddings require extra planning on your part, because many of your guests may be unfamiliar with the area. Reserve a block of rooms so that they can all stay in the same hotel. Organize the activities, rather than leaving your guests to make their own plans.

Theme Weddings

Strictly speaking, a "theme wedding" is one in which every detail is faithfully tied into a central theme. More commonly, we see touches of a theme, which adds ambiance and charm without the restrictions. Decorations, menu, music, and even transportation can all reflect the theme of the wedding.

Many Christmas weddings take on a holiday theme. Also popular is the beach theme for an outdoor wedding. Weddings can take their cue from historical periods, such as Victorian times. They can be themed to geographical locations, such as Hawaii. Even colors can provide the inspiration, such as a black and white wedding.

Theme weddings will be covered in more detail in Chapter 16.

Canceling the Wedding

As unpleasant as it is, engagements occasionally get broken. It is better to break an engagement than to go through a divorce.

Tell friends and family first, either by telephone or by note. You do not need to explain why you have ended your engagement. You must also notify anyone you have contracted for the wedding, such as caterers, florists, etc. Be prepared to lose your deposits.

There is still some debate over whether the engagement ring should be returned. Some say, "Yes, no engagement means no ring." Others say, "No, it was a gift." If the ring was an heirloom from the groom's family, it *must* be returned.

If the invitations have already been sent out, a printed announcement is mailed to each invited guest. The announcement is issued by whoever issued the invitations:

Mr. and Mrs. James Johnson regret that the marriage of their daughter, Susan, will not take place.

Again, no explanation is necessary. If time does not permit announcements, guests can be notified by telephone.

All shower and wedding gifts that have been received must be returned. Take the time to write a small note, thanking the giver for their generosity.

Postponing the Wedding

If the wedding is to be postponed, announcements are sent to the invited guests. It is not necessary to provide any explanation, although it is customary to do so, such as:

Due to a death in the immediate family, the wedding of Susan Johnson and John Hall will be postponed until a later date.

Wedding gifts are kept, and thank-you cards written as usual. If the new date has already been set, guests can be notified at the same time. See Chapter 5 for the correct wording. Otherwise, keep everyone up-to-date as new plans unfold.

Wedding Insurance

Wedding insurance ensures that you will be reimbursed financially if something beyond your control threatens to ruin your wedding day.

Policies (and therefore premiums) vary widely, so read the fine print and communicate openly with your insurance broker. Two things are not covered: if either the bride or groom cancels the engagement, or if a pregnant bride goes into labor within a certain time before the wedding. Other than these, many items are covered, such as:

- Lost deposits due to a vendor going out of business
- Damage to the wedding gown
- Loss or damage of rented items
- Stolen wedding gifts
- Illness or injury, necessitating the postponement of the wedding and loss of deposits
- Vendor no-show, necessitating the last-minute hiring of a replacement at a higher fee, and the reimbursement of deposits made
- The costs of rescheduling due to weather
- Last-minute job relocation, necessitating the cancellation of the wedding plans made to that point
- Damage to film or videotape

In the majority of these cases, the insurance will cover the costs of rescheduling the wedding. In the case of photographs and video, you will be covered for the costs of "restaging." This includes the cost of replacement flowers, wedding cake, etc.

It cannot be stressed enough: be sure you know exactly what is (and is not) included in your policy before you sign. That way, you will have the coverage you need.

Origins of Popular Wedding Customs

Many wedding customs have their beginnings rooted in superstition. Others have come down to us from ancient times. If you examine the origins of some of these old customs, you may discover a way to include them in your own wedding, and perhaps set a new family tradition.

During ancient times, marriage was by capture. The groom would arrive at the bride's home with his best man and groomsmen to help him in case the bride's father and brothers tried to stop them. To confuse the men, the bride would assemble a group of maids, dressed alike. To give the bride's family time to cool down, the groom took her away for a period of a month, during which time they would drink a honeyed wine called "meade," hence the honeymoon.

When Queen Victoria married her beloved Prince Albert in 1820, she wore a white gown. Before then, white was considered the color of purity and virtue, but it was not associated with brides. It was usual for a bride to be married in her Sunday best. Queen Victoria also revived the ancient bridal custom of carrying orange blossoms. The orange tree is the only one to bear its flowers and fruit at the same time, making it an ancient symbol of beauty and fertility.

The wedding shower began in Holland, where a poor miller's daughter wanted to marry. Her friends gathered with gifts to form her dowry.

Since ancient times, it has been believed that the third finger of the left hand contained a vein that leads directly to the heart. The wedding band is a continuous circle with no beginning or end, symbolizing eternity. Maximilian of Austria gave the first diamond engagement ring to Mary of Burgundy in 1477.

The engagement period was a time for the families of the bride and groom to complete the transfer of ownership of the bride from her father to her husband.

The garter has its beginnings in the oldest order of knighthood in Europe, the Order of the Garter. The ring bearer also emerged here, but originally carried the bride's train.

June is the feast month of Juno, the Roman goddess of marriage. Couples married in her month had a marriage blessed by her.

Ancient seclusion rites are the basis for our lighthearted custom of preventing the groom from seeing the bride before the wedding.

Every bride knows the old rhyme, "Something old, something new, something borrowed, something blue." There are many interpretations, but traditionally something old meant the continuity of marriage and family life. Something new was hope for the future. Something borrowed was the happiness of others and something blue represented the color of loyalty and fidelity.

The wedding cake has symbolized many things over the centuries, including the bounty of the harvest and a rich sweet life.

In ancient Rome, a kiss was the only legal bond.

The bride's handkerchief was to catch the bride's tears of joy, which were lucky and meant that she would never shed another tear.

The crushing of a glass at a Jewish wedding has been given several meanings, from the destruction of the temple in Jerusalem to the end of the bride's old life.

An aisle runner was used to protect the bride and the wedding party from the evil spirits who lived under the floorboards. The runner was white, the path of purity.

Setting the Date

There are many factors to consider before setting a date for your wedding. Perhaps you have a special anniversary, such as the day you met or your first date. This is a great starting point, but before you mark the calendar, consider the following:

- Has the clergy of your church already booked a wedding for that date?
- Does the date fall during busy wedding months? If so, you may have to book the venue a year or more in advance.
- Will the date fall on a long weekend? Some guests find this to be an advantage, especially if they must travel to attend your wedding. Your local friends may think that your wedding is keeping them stuck in town.
- Does the date coincide with a religious holiday? If so, the clergy may not be available.
- Does the date coincide with a sad anniversary, such as the death of a loved one?
- Is this a good time for both of you to book time off work?
- Consider your honeymoon plans. Does the date mean that you will arrive on your favorite tropical island in the middle of hurricane season?
- Carefully consider the day of the week, as well as the time of the day. For instance: Can you get substantial discounts for booking on a day other than Saturday? Will your guests have to deal with rush-hour traffic on their way to the wedding?

This may be a good time to remind you that when you book your ceremony, you should also book your rehearsal the night before.

Wedding Web Sites

Many of today's couples keep friends and family up-to-date by their wedding blog. You can also take advantage of the many wedding-planning sites which offer "wed sites," often free of charge. You will be given a password, and your wedding guests can visit it as often as they wish. Consider putting the following onto your wedding site:

- The date, time, and location of the wedding
- Your pictures and short biographies
- Links to the reception and ceremony sites
- Links to any tourist attractions in the area
- Links to hotels and their reservation desks
- Links to your gift registries
- An update in which you keep your guests abreast of all news as it happens
- Anything else your guests should know

Why Every Bride Should Hire a Wedding Planner

A wedding planner is both a luxury and a necessity. Much work will go into creating the wedding of your dreams; it is a luxury to have someone to do that work for you.

If you need help planning the details, your wedding planner will be your best ally as you negotiate with vendors and wade your way through schedules, stores, and budgets. Perhaps you have planned some parts of your wedding and need help with others. Your wedding planner can assist you where you need it most. If you want to plan the wedding yourself, hire a wedding planner to be on hand the day of the ceremony to look after things at the church and reception. This is called "coordinating" the wedding. That way, you are free to enjoy your guests and your new husband.

You will be asked for a non-refundable deposit, which will hold the date and cover the work that she does on your behalf until she is paid in full. Although she will charge for her services, her knowledge of the vendors and her ability to "do it right the first time" will actually save you money.

Ask about her credentials; preferably she will be certified. Find out how she works with the vendors and who pays her. If she takes commissions from the vendors or receives any referral fees, hire a different planner. You want someone who has no conflict of interest. Your wedding planner should work for you alone.

Have everything spelled out clearly in a contract or letter of agreement. Find out about fees, deposits, and cancellation policies. Be sure the contract lists in detail what her duties are to include.

Planning Calendars

Use a planning calendar, one month per page, to schedule everything that must be done in the months leading up to the wedding.

A commercially printed calendar will serve the purpose, or custom-design a calendar on your computer.

Immediately enter the wedding date. Using the "Bride's Timeline and Checklist" and the "Groom's Timeline and Checklist" found at the end of this chapter, pencil in the tasks that must be done in certain months. When appointments have been booked and confirmed, erase the pencil, and write the times and details in ink. Use the margins to make notes.

Showers

As a rule, the immediate families do not host wedding showers, although many do. It is better for a friend, usually the maid of honor, to plan the shower.

Certain people *must* receive shower invitations, including the mothers of the bride and groom, the bridesmaids and maid of honor, the mothers of the flower girl and the ring bearer, and the sisters of the bride and groom. Under no circumstances should a shower invitation be sent to someone who has not been invited to the wedding.

It has become a trend to give "theme showers." These include kitchen, garden, bathroom, bar, pantry, and lingerie showers. Many couples enjoy attending "Jack and Jill" showers, in which the bride and groom are both showered with gifts by their male and female friends. Many guests choose shower gifts from the list at the Bridal Registry, so register for smaller items as well as the usual registry gifts.

A handwritten thank-you note is mandatory. Early in your engagement is the perfect time to get into the habit of promptly writing and keeping up with these notes! Don't forget a special note to thank the hostess.

Other Parties

It has become a custom for the bride and groom to each have a night out with their friends just before the wedding. These have earned a reputation for being rowdy affairs, with strippers and too much drinking. It is now becoming fashionable to drink responsibly, and to have much tamer get-togethers. Grooms are much more likely to go golfing with their friends than to bars. The groom presents his attendants with thank-you gifts at this time, and they will give him their gift. Toward the end of the evening, the groom proposes a toast to the bride, which is responded to by those in attendance.

The bride enjoys a girls' night out, often called "bachelorette party." It can be dinner or an evening at the theatre. As well, she often gets together for lunch with her bridesmaids and maid of honor, during which gifts are exchanged. This get-together can be held any time, but is usually scheduled a week or so before the wedding.

If guests will be attending from out of town, it is a nice gesture to host a little party for them. This is held the night before the wedding, and can be hosted by anyone who is not at the rehearsal dinner. The intention is two-fold: it entertains guests who may be unfamiliar with the location, and it relieves the bride's mother, who has so much to do at this point.

The Wedding at a Glance

WEDDING DATE

CEREMONY LOCATION

Address
Telephone
Fax
E-mail
Contact person

CEREMONY TIME

OFFICIANT

Name
Telephone
E-mail

NUMBER OF GUESTS

RECEPTION LOCATION

Address
Telephone
Fax
E-mail
Web site
Contact person

RECEPTION TIME

NUMBER OF GUESTS

INVITATIONS

Ordered from
Telephone
Contact person

BEST MAN

Name
Address
Telephone
E-mail

USHER 1

Name
Address
Telephone
E-mail

USHER 2

Name
Address
Telephone
E-mail

USHER 3

Name
Address
Telephone
E-mail

MAID OF HONOR

Name
Address

Telephone
E-mail

BRIDESMAID 1

Name
Address
Telephone
E-mail

BRIDESMAID 2

Name
Address
Telephone
E-mail

BRIDESMAID 3

Name
Address
Telephone
E-mail

FLOWER GIRL

Name
Address
Telephone
E-mail

RING BEARER

Name
Address
Telephone
E-mail

MARRIAGE LICENSE OFFICE

Address
Telephone
Hours
Fee

ORGANIST

Name
Telephone
E-mail

SOLOIST

Name
Telephone
E-mail

WEDDING PLANNER

Name
Address
Telephone
E-mail

JEWELER

Name
Address
Telephone
E-mail
Contact person

TRANSPORTATION

Name
Address

Telephone
E-mail
Contact person

FLORIST

Name
Address
Telephone
E-mail
Contact person

PHOTOGRAPHY AND VIDEO

Name
Address
Telephone
E-mail
Contact person

CATERER

Name
Address
Telephone
E-mail
Contact person

WEDDING CAKE

Baker
Address
Telephone
E-mail
Contact person

DISC JOCKEY

Name
Address
Telephone
E-mail
Contact person

FORMAL WEAR

Name
Address
Telephone
E-mail
Contact person

BRIDAL BOUTIQUE

Name Address
Telephone
E-mail
Contact person

Budget Master List

WEDDING FASHIONS

Bride's gown
Veil and headpiece
Lingerie
Shoes
Accessories
Jewelry
Groom's tuxedo
Accessories
Shoes

Total

CEREMONY

Clergy fees
Organist
Site rental
Bride's wedding ring
Groom's wedding ring
Marriage license

Total

RECEPTION

Site rental
Caterer/food
Bar
Wedding cake
Decorations
Music

Total

FLOWERS

Church decorations
Bride's bouquet
Bridesmaids' bouquets
Maid of honor's bouquet
Flower girl's basket
Ring bearer's pillow
Groom's boutonniere
Ushers'/Best man's boutonnieres
Ring bearer's boutonniere
Fathers'/Grandfathers' boutonnieres
Mothers'/Grandmothers' corsages
Other boutonnieres or corsages
Reception flowers

Total

STATIONERY

Invitations
Announcements
Response cards
Pew cards
Place cards
Programs
Thank-you notes
Napkins

Total

PHOTOGRAPHY

Photographer
Prints
Albums
Video

Total

TRANSPORTATION

Limousines
Parking
Out-of-town guests

Total

GIFTS

Bride's attendant gifts
Groom's attendant gifts
Bride's gift to the groom
Groom's gift to the bride
Favors for guests

Total

MISCELLANEOUS

Wedding planner
Accommodation for out-of-town guests
Bridesmaids' lunch

Total

REHEARSAL DINNER

Food
Site rental
Clothing
Flowers
Bar
Decorations
Music

Total

HONEYMOON

Travel
Accommodation

Clothing
Passports
Luggage
Food
Souvenirs

Total

GRAND TOTAL

Bride's Timeline and Checklist

12 MONTHS BEFORE THE WEDDING

- Decide on style, colors, and formality
- Set wedding budget
- Choose ceremony site; book date
- Choose reception site; book date
- Book tent rental if ceremony or reception will be outdoors
- Book caterer if reception venue does not have an in-house caterer
- Begin planning menu
- Book photographer
- Book videographer
- Book DJ or musicians

9 MONTHS BEFORE THE WEDDING

- Visit clergy with fiancé; discuss writing your own vows
- Choose attendants
- Order wedding gown
- Start guest list
- Make honeymoon plans

6 MONTHS BEFORE THE WEDDING

- Order accessories
- Book limousines
- Order attendants' dresses
- Order invitations and enclosures, announcements
- Finalize honeymoon plans
- Order flowers for the ceremony and reception

3 MONTHS BEFORE THE WEDDING

- Begin addressing invitations
- Have the groom choose formal rentals
- Meet with church organist
- Arrange for a liquor license and order liquor, beer, wine, and champagne for the reception (if not available through reception venue)
- Order wedding rings
- Order wedding cake
- Book hair, nails, and makeup
- Book a block of rooms for out-of-town guests
- Finalize menu

6 TO 8 WEEKS BEFORE THE WEDDING

- Mail invitations
- Have dress fittings for your gown and attendants' dresses
- Buy gifts for your attendants and your groom
- Send announcement to newspaper
- Plan bridesmaids' lunch
- Mail invitations
- Plan rehearsal and rehearsal party
- Finalize plans with florist, photographer, videographer
- Pick up rings

2 WEEKS BEFORE THE WEDDING

- Finalize arrangements with caterer
- Go with your fiancé to get the marriage license
- Address announcements for mailing after the ceremony
- Confirm all honeymoon plans
- Contact photographer, videographer, and DJ with request lists
- Arrange for pick-up of your gown and bridesmaids' dresses

1 WEEK BEFORE THE WEDDING

- Lunch with bridesmaids

- Attend bachelorette party
- Contact caterer with final head count
- Provide attendants and clergy with details of rehearsal dinner
- Check with each vendor regarding final details
- Write checks to be put in envelopes and distributed on the wedding day
- Begin packing for honeymoon

THE NIGHT BEFORE THE WEDDING

- Rehearsal and rehearsal dinner
- Give the envelopes with checks to the person who will hand them out
- Pack going-away outfit
- Finish packing for honeymoon
- Get a good night's sleep!

Groom's Timeline and Checklist

12 MONTHS BEFORE THE WEDDING

- Pick out bride's engagement ring
- Discuss your share of wedding expenses with the bride and her family
- Choose ceremony site with fiancée
- Choose reception site with fiancée

9 MONTHS BEFORE THE WEDDING

- Visit clergy with fiancée; discuss writing your own vows
- Choose best man and ushers
- Go with fiancée to register for gifts
- Start guest list
- Make honeymoon plans with fiancée

6 MONTHS BEFORE THE WEDDING

- Book limousine to take you and the best man to the ceremony, if he will not be driving
- Finalize honeymoon plans

3 MONTHS BEFORE THE WEDDING

- Choose formal rentals
- Have best man and ushers choose formal rentals
- Go with fiancée to meet church organist
- Order wedding rings
- Book a block of hotel rooms for out-of-town guests

6 TO 8 WEEKS BEFORE THE WEDDING

- Buy gifts for best man and ushers and your bride
- Plan rehearsal and rehearsal dinner
- Pick up rings

2 WEEKS BEFORE THE WEDDING

- Go with your fiancée to get the marriage license
- Arrange for transportation for you and your bride after reception
- Confirm honeymoon reservations

1 WEEK BEFORE THE WEDDING

- Arrange for pickup of rented formal wear
- Attend bachelor's party
- Begin packing for honeymoon
- Purchase traveler's checks
- Provide best man and ushers with the details of rehearsal dinner
- Be sure ushers are aware of any special seating arrangements

THE NIGHT BEFORE THE WEDDING

- Rehearsal and rehearsal dinner
- Give envelope with clergy's fees to the best man
- Finish packing for honeymoon
- Get a good night's sleep!

For Your Notes

CHAPTER 2

The Wedding Party

The Best Man

The best man is usually the groom's best friend, his brother, or even his father. He has a very important role to play in planning the wedding and making sure the day runs smoothly. Among his responsibilities are:

- Get the groom to the church on time
- Hold the bride's ring until the appropriate place in the ceremony
- Make sure the groom has the marriage license, and sign it as a witness to the marriage
- Present the officiant's fee
- Drive the bride and groom from the ceremony to the reception and from the reception (if limousines will not be used)
- Plan the bachelor party
- Attend the rehearsal and rehearsal dinner
- Collect money from the groomsmen and buy joint gift for the groom

- Pick up rented formal wear and return it on time
- Propose a toast at the reception
- Read congratulatory telegrams
- Help the groom change to leave the reception
- Pay for his own formal wear

The Maid of Honor

The maid of honor is usually the best friend or sister of the bride. If she is married, she is referred to as a "matron of honor." Her duties include:

- Host a bridal shower
- Help the bride dress for the ceremony and after the reception
- Hold the bride's bouquet and the groom's ring during the ceremony
- Sign the marriage license as a witness to the marriage
- Adjust the bride's train and veil after the processional and recessional
- Attend the rehearsal and rehearsal dinner
- Deliver the bride's gown to her home after the reception
- Collect money from the bridesmaids and buy joint gift for the bride
- Plan bachelorette party
- Attend lunch with bride and bridesmaids

- Pay for her own attire

The Groomsmen (or Ushers)

The ushers or groomsmen will seat the guests as they arrive at the church. They are chosen from among the groom's friends and relatives. He can also make the gesture of asking the bride's brothers. The oldest of the group will be designated "Head Usher." He will seat the mothers of the bride and groom, with one exception–if one of the other ushers is a brother of the bride or groom, he will seat his own mother.

The ushers will seat the bride's friends and family on the left and groom's on the right (reversed for the Jewish ceremony). Mutual friends can be seated on whichever side has fewer guests. The groom should choose one usher for every fifty guests. There should be an equal number of bridesmaids and groomsmen. The duties of the ushers are:

- Attend bachelor party
- Contribute to groom's gift
- Attend rehearsal and rehearsal dinner
- Seat guests
- Distribute programs and driving directions to the reception venue
- Pull the aisle runner
- Transport bridesmaids from the ceremony to the reception
- Dance with single women at the reception
- Pay for their own formal wear

The Bridesmaids

The bridesmaids have very few official duties. They are decoration, a custom left over from ancient times. Nevertheless, it is an honor to be asked to be in the wedding party. The bride chooses her bridesmaids from among her friends and family. As a gesture, she may include the sisters of the groom. The bridesmaids are expected to:

- Attend showers and parties
- Contribute to the gift for the bride
- Attend the rehearsal and rehearsal dinner
- Take part in the processional and recessional
- Take part in the receiving line
- Pay for their own attire

The Flower Girl

The flower girl is between the ages of four and eight; if she is an older girl, she will be a junior bridesmaid. Her function is to carry a basket of rose petals, which she will scatter on the aisle before the bride, although she often carries a small basket of flowers instead.

Her dress can be white or ivory; the satin sash can match the bridesmaids' dresses. It is a lovely idea to have the young daughter of the bride or groom as the flower girl.

You can have two flower girls, especially if you are in the position of having to choose between two girls and disappointing one of them. Have them walk down the aisle together with the ring bearer between them.

The flower girl has the option of standing at the altar or sitting with her parents. If she does not stand at the altar, she leaves the church with her parents. She does not return to the altar to take part in the recessional.

The flower girl will attend the rehearsal (the dinner is at the discretion of her parents), but she is not expected to stand in the receiving line.

The Ring Bearer

The ring bearer is between the ages of four and eight; an older boy is a junior usher. He will be dressed in a suit or in a tuxedo to match the ushers.

The ring bearer will accompany the flower girl in the processional, carrying a satin pillow onto which the wedding rings are tied. Often the rings are imitations; the real rings are safely in the care of the best man and maid of honor. If the real rings are used, they must be *securely* tied and removed by the best man as soon as they reach the altar. Have him carry a pair of nail scissors to make this easier.

As with the flower girl, the ring bearer has the option of standing at the altar or sitting with his parents. If he does not stand at the altar, he leaves the church with his parents. He does not return to the altar to take part in the recessional.

The ring bearer will attend the rehearsal (the dinner is at the discretion of his parents), but he is not expected to stand in the receiving line.

Don't be alarmed if a flower girl or ring bearer gets a last-minute case of stage fright. Have a bridesmaid ready to take the small child by the hand. If there are tears, the child can sit in the pews with his or her parents. The guests will understand, and this should be handled without causing the child embarrassment.

Pages and Train Bearers

These are seen only in the largest formal weddings. Pages are young boys who have various duties; they can serve as altar boys or attend the guest book. If the boy is old enough, he may be able to light the candles.

The train bearer is responsible for the bride's train. Usually this job is performed by a young boy, although a girl may also fill the role. The train bearer follows the bride during the processional, holding her train just slightly off the ground. For an extremely formal wedding in which the bride's train is very long, two identically-dressed train bearers can be used.

The Mother of the Bride

The bride's mother is the hostess at the reception and the most honored guest at the wedding. If she and the bride's father are divorced, she still takes the role, even if his second wife is present.

She is the last to be seated before the ceremony, by the head usher or a groomsman who is a family member. If she and the bride's father are divorced, she sits in the front pew with her new husband; he and his new wife sit in the third pew.

The mothers of the bride and groom may light the unity candle after the candle lighters have left the altar area and prior to the entrance of the wedding party.

The bride's mother makes reservations for out-of-town guests invited by her family. She stands at the front of the receiving line, and is the first to greet guests. She introduces her friends and family to the groom's mother.

The Mother of the Groom

The groom's mother will be escorted down the aisle to the first pew, right-hand side, by the head usher or a groomsman who is a family member. Occasionally, a groom may wish to escort his mother down the aisle. As the groom's mother is escorted to her seat, her husband follows behind. If the parents are divorced, the father of the groom will have been seated previously in the third pew.

The groom's mother provides the bride's mother with the names and complete addresses for wedding invitations, and chooses a dress that is in keeping with the formality of the bride's mother.

She and her husband host the rehearsal dinner, and stand in the receiving line, greeting guests and introducing their friends and family to the bride and her family.

Wedding Party Information

Maid of Honor:

Name

Address

Telephone

Email

Best Man:

Name

Address

Telephone

Email

Bridesmaid:

Name

Address

Telephone

Email

Bridesmaid:

Name

Address

Telephone

Email

Bridesmaid:

Name

Address

Telephone

Email

Bridesmaid:

Name

Address

Telephone

E-mail

Bridesmaid:

Name

Address

Telephone

Email

Groomsman:

Name

Address

Telephone

Email

Groomsman:

Name

Address

Telephone

E-mail

Groomsman:

Name

Address

Telephone

E-mail

Groomsman:

Name

Address

Telephone

Email

Groomsman:

Name

Address

Telephone

Email

Flower Girl:

Name

Address

Telephone

Ring Bearer:

Name

Address

Telephone

For Your Notes

CHAPTER 3

Wedding Fashions

Bridal Boutiques

Bridal boutiques are the second most expensive way to find a wedding dress, next to having one custom-made. If you simply *must* economize in this category, you can go to a bridal warehouse or outlet, or even a department store. However, you will not find the quality of service that a bridal boutique offers. At the lesser stores, there is no alteration service, there are often stains and rips in the gowns, and the sales staff is less knowledgeable.

Book your appointment for a weeknight, as weekends are busier. Allow nine months to order and alter the gown. The bare *minimum* amount of time involved (if few alterations are required) is six months.

The deposit (usually fifty percent) is best paid with a credit card, as you may have some recourse if the dress is not delivered. Once the order has been placed with the manufacturer, it cannot be canceled. Choose a store with a five-day cancellation policy. Keep all receipts, and get all prices in writing.

More expensive alterations will be needed on a more ornate gown. Order to a specific manufacturer. Sizes can differ by as much as an inch and a half.

You will often get a discount if you order your gown and the bridesmaids' dresses from the same shop. The same applies to the mothers and the flower girl.

Try on several different styles, even if you have a preference. Traditional styles are never out of date. The biggest mistake many brides make is to find the "perfect" gown but keep looking for something even more perfect. Bring a camera and ask if you can take a picture. Many stores forbid it, to avoid you having the gown copied elsewhere. After you've placed a deposit, you will probably be allowed to take a photo.

Custom-Made Gowns

If you will be having your wedding gown custom-made, be prepared to pay two to three times more than if you bought a gown at a bridal boutique. But just imagine how you'll feel as you walk down the aisle in a one-of-a-kind designer original!

The first step is to have a consultation with the dressmaker. She will analyze your body type and listen as you describe the dress you have in mind. If you have pictures of design details you like, all the better. You will look at swatches to choose the fabric and lace. The dressmaker will sketch the final design, take your measurements, and order the fabric.

A pattern will be made from muslin (an inexpensive fabric) and will be modified and altered until it is perfect. When you arrive for your muslin fittings, wear the lingerie and shoes that you will wear with the wedding gown. After the muslin version looks and fits perfectly it will be taken apart and used as the pattern for your gown.

Be prepared for at least one fitting of the finished gown. Again, lingerie and shoes make a difference in the way the gown will look and fit.

A Wedding Gown to Flatter Every Figure

Every bride wants to look her best on her wedding day, and fortunately there is a wedding gown to let you accentuate your best features and play down the ones you want to hide.

Small hips: Add to the hip while subtracting from the upper part of the body. A very full skirt will do the trick. A gown with simple sleeves and a V-neckline will not attract the eye upward.

Large hips: Attract attention to the upper part of the body. This can be done by accentuating the bust area with a strapless gown, or by adding extra detail to the top of the gown. Consider such things as padded shoulders, elaborate necklines, and beading or lace on the bodice.

Small waist: A princess waistline or a natural waistline will show off your small waist. Have a tightly fitting bodice and a full skirt.

Sexy legs: Wear a shorter dress, or have a slit in the skirt.

Lovely shoulders: Bare them with a strapless gown, or one that features a portrait neckline.

Lovely back: Many fabulous backless gowns feature extra detail at the back. After all, your back is what your guests see during the ceremony. Let several strands of pearls fall down your back.

Heavy arms: Draw attention away from the arms and toward the waist, using bustles, full skirts, or peplums. Be sure the sleeves are not puffy, and that the shoulders are not padded. Avoid strapless or off-the-shoulder styles.

Thin arms: Wear long sleeves; if you want short sleeves make them full or puffy. Elbow-length gloves were made for you!

Lovely hands: Show them off with long sleeves that come to a point.

Lovely neck: Attract attention by using an elegant neckline.

Too thin: Add fullness to the bodice area with extra detailing, beading, and appliqués. Choose a style with a very full skirt. A princess waistline should work very well for you. The best fabrics are "dimensional," such as embroidered lace.

Too heavy: Avoid heavy beading and detailing, and fabrics such as satin and velvet. Choose a simple style and avoid overly full skirts.

Too short: Don't be overpowered with heavy fabrics and too much detailing. Emphasize vertical lines and keep the detailing small in scale.

Too tall: Add width. Incorporate horizontal lines and add details such as a picture hat.

Wedding Fabrics

Satin: A fabric characterized by its smooth and shiny surface

Velvet: A thick, soft fabric, produced by weaving loops and shearing the top surface; made of cotton, silk, or synthetic fiber

Taffeta: A smooth and shiny fabric with a crisp feeling

Crepe: A polyester blend with a tight weave

Brocade: A cotton blend with a raised design

Jacquard: A heavy satin fabric with a raised design

Tulle: Fine sheer netting, made of cotton, nylon, rayon, or silk; used for veils

Silk: A natural fiber, very luxurious to the touch

Shantung: Slubs and imperfections; otherwise, similar to raw silk

Chiffon: A sheer tissue-like fabric of silk or synthetic fibers

Point d'Esprit: A cotton, silk, or rayon net fabric, showing woven dots throughout

Eyelet: A silk, cotton, or polyester fabric, showing embroidered holes around the edges

Batiste: A sheer fabric of cotton or a cotton blend, most suitable for summer

Organdy: A silk fabric, very fine, with a stiff finish

Organza: A thin, finely-woven summer fabric with a stiff and crisp texture; made of silk, cotton, or synthetics; also available as embroidered organza

Voile: A cotton or cotton/polyester blend with a light and open weave

Illusion: Transparent tulle, used for veils or to add interest to necklines

Charmeuse: A soft weave, semi-lustrous, lighter than satin but otherwise similar

Peau de Soie: A winter fabric in a dull satiny finish

Moire: A heavy fabric with an irregular wavelike finish

Wedding Laces

Battenberg: A heavier lace with the feeling of a Renaissance fabric

Brussels: Raised lace resembling a flower; very delicate with subtle patterns; also called "daisy lace"

Alencon: A design of leaves and rose clusters on a net background, often with an "eyelash" edge

Chantilly: Similar to Alencon lace, but without the net; very expensive

Venise: A roseleaf pattern featuring heavy stitching and a three-dimensional effect

Lyon: A fine lace of floral patterns

Cluny: A lace of fine linen thread, featuring wheel or wheat designs

Schiffli: A machine-made lace of a cotton/polyester blend

Guipure: Lace with a bold pattern and few connective stitches

Necklines

At any given time, certain styles and features are more prevalent. However, it is usually possible to find wedding gowns with traditional styling that are not "in style" at the moment.

Band: An upright collar, giving the gown a Victorian look

Scoop: A very low, rounded neckline

Off-the-shoulder: Short sleeve that sits below the shoulder, covering part of the upper arm but baring the shoulders

Décolletage: An off-the-shoulder neckline, plunging into a low-cut V-shape

High collar: As the name implies, a collar that extends to just below the jaw line

Illusion neckline: A high neckline formed of lace or net, beginning at the bust line

Jewel: A very high, rounded neckline

Bertha collar: A "cape" of fabric or lace ruffles on the neckline

Spaghetti straps: Narrow shoulder straps on an otherwise strapless gown

Portrait: A very elegant neckline, so-named because it "frames" the face and shoulders

Queen Elizabeth collar: High at the back, flowing down to a V-front

Sabrina: Popularized by Audrey Hepburn; crosses from shoulder to shoulder along the collarbone

Bateau: Slightly lower than the Sabrina neckline; sits just below the collar-bone; extends shoulder-to-shoulder, and can expose the shoulders, if desired

Halter: Straps run from the bodice around the neck

Square neckline: Straight on the sides and across the bottom; often low-cut

Strapless: Shoulders are completely bare; sometimes worn with a jacket during the ceremony

Sweetheart: Quite open and named for its resemblance to a heart

V-neck: Comes to a point at the bottom; many variations, including a scalloped version

Queen Anne: High at the back and sides; opens at the front to resemble a sweetheart neckline

Waistlines

Empire: Above the natural waistline, sometimes with an upward curve toward the center

Blouson: Full and billowing at the top, gathered closely at the waistline

Dropped: Several inches below the natural waistline

Basque: About two inches below the natural waistline, usually ending in a point at the center

Cummerbund: Gathered fabric, similar to that found in men's formal wear

Sleeves

Fitted: A set-in sleeve with no fullness, either long or short

Fitted point or long point: A fitted sleeve that ends in a point on the hand

Gauntlet: A detachable lace that is worn instead of gloves; covers the wrist and the forearm

Balloon: A large puffy sleeve, extending to the elbow

Pouf: A full sleeve that ends at the elbow; can also be worn off the shoulder

Cap: A fitted sleeve that barely covers the shoulders

Leg-o-Mutton: A sleeve that is full to the elbow, tapering to a fit at the wrist

Gibson: A short version of the leg-o-mutton

Bow: A sleeve that consists of fabric loops creating a large bow; also called "butterfly"

Dolman: A sleeve with a shoulder-to-waist width, gathered at the wrist

Juliette: A long sleeve with a slight puff at the top and fitted on the forearm

Bishop: A very full long sleeve, gathered at the wrist, usually in a cuff

Hemlines

Street length: Barely covering the knees

Intermission: Between the knees and the ankles

Mini: Above the knees

Graduated: Mid-calf at the front and floor-length at the back

Tea length: Several inches above the ankles

Ballet length: Just above the ankles

Floor length: A half-inch to an inch-and-a-half off the floor

Train Lengths

Watteau: A train that attaches at the shoulders

Detachable: A train that is removable for ease of movement at the reception

Royal: A train that extends nine feet from the waist

Cathedral: A train that extends six feet from the waist

Chapel: A train that extends four to five feet from the waist

Court: A train that extends three feet from the waist

Sweep: A train that barely sweeps the floor

Skirt Details

Bustle: Fullness at the back, created with padding or a wire frame. Some trains can also be bustled for freedom of movement

Peplum: A short flounce, gathered at the waistline

Accordion Pleats: Sharp-edged pleats resembling an accordion

Fan-Back: An otherwise smooth skirt with accordion pleats in the back only

Pannier: Gathered fabric over the hips

Tails: Two panels of fabric that flow from the waist at the back

Tiers: Various lengths in layers

Drape: Fullness added by gathering extra fabric at the seams

Fishtail: An additional panel sewn into the back of the skirt

Decoration

Matte sequin: A white-backed sequin

Aurora Borealis sequin (AB): Clear and multicolored

Iridescent sequin: White-backed and multicolored

Iridescent pearl: A pearl with a multicolored shine

Bugle pearl: A teardrop-shaped pearl

Seed pearls: Small pearls, round and resembling seeds

Windows Patterns cut into the fabric and filled with illusion

Appliqués: Lace, sometimes beaded or sequined, sewn to the fabric

Rosettes: Fabric roses

Not All White is White

There are many different "whites," and you can only tell the difference between them by seeing them side-by-side. Not surprisingly, different whites look better with different skin tones.

Champagne white has a very subtle pink undertone. It is a "warm" white, and looks good on brides with yellow skin tones.

Eggshell white is a little creamy, but lighter than ivory. It's perfect for brides with fair skin, but does not look good with yellow skin tones.

Stark white is just as its name implies. If you have yellow skin tones, this one's for you.

Natural white is warmer than stark white, and is good if your skin is a pink tone. If your skin is dark, you can wear all of the whites and look great!

Gloves

The length of the bride's gloves depends on the formality and style of her gown; the more formal the gown, the longer the glove. With a sleeveless or strapless gown, the only suitable gloves will be elbow-length. For an informal short-sleeved gown, short gloves are appropriate. Gloves are not worn with a long-sleeved gown.

Long gloves that reach the elbow are called, naturally, elbow length, while opera length gloves extend to the upper arm. Try on several glove styles while trying on gowns.

Bridesmaids and mothers can wear gloves that have been dyed to match their gowns, or white gloves.

Gloves are removed only for eating. The stitches of the ring finger are split so that the wedding ring can be put on without removing the glove.

Jewelry

This is certainly a time when less is more! A few quality pieces on the small side are best. Pearls are traditionally worn as wedding jewelry. Stones are fine as long as they are not brightly colored, too large, or flashy. Diamonds, always!

Necklaces should be chosen to flatter the neckline of your gown, earrings to flatter your headpiece and veil.

This is the best time to plan your "something old" or "something borrowed," in the form of an heirloom piece. Watches are not appropriate with wedding attire.

Jewelry can unify the look of your bridesmaids. Simple pearls and gold are always in the best of taste. Choose the bridesmaids' jewelry as your gift to them.

Shoes

The most important thing is comfort. You will be standing for long periods of time and dancing the night away, so be sure your shoes fit well and are the correct heel height for you. You have many style choices:

Pump: A closed shoe which slips on

Sling back: A strap which fastens across the back of the heel

Sandal: An open shoe with straps

Flat: A shoe with the heel less than half an inch high

Ballet slipper: A flat shoe, often with ribbons, made of soft material

Break in your shoes before the wedding. Scuff the soles with sandpaper so that you won't slip and fall while dancing or walking up the aisle. The rest of the wedding party should do the same.

Bridesmaids' shoes are often dyed to match their dresses. They are seldom worn again, so thoughtful brides allow the girls to choose shoes in black, white, gold, or silver (they must all be the same color), and in their own heel height.

Veils

The veil itself is attached to a tiara, Juliette cap, floral comb, or floral wreath. Veils are described according to their length.

Fly-away: A short veil, usually worn with a less formal gown; multi-layer veil that brushes the shoulders

Mantilla: A circular piece of lace, held in place by a comb

Fountain: A veil which is gathered at the top of the head and cascades around the face

Blusher: A short veil, worn over the bride's face during the processional

Birdcage: A stationary veil, pinned at the top of the head and falling to just below the chin

Chapel length: A veil which falls approximately seven to eight feet from the headpiece

Cathedral length: A veil which falls approximately ten to eleven feet from the headpiece

Ballet length: A veil which falls to the ankle; also called "waltz length"

Fingertip length: Literally, to the level of the fingertips when the arms are held straight down at the sides

Pouf: A small gathered veil attached to a headpiece

Veils are usually made of a sheer fabric called illusion or tulle, but can also be made from the following:

English net: A round weave, as opposed to the small diamond weave of tulle

Russian: A large diamond weave

Organza: In this case, a lace made of organza

Point d'Esprit: Dots within the illusion set at orderly intervals

Lingerie

The lingerie you wear on your wedding day will provide the foundation necessary to make your wedding gown look its best. It can change the way your dress fits, so purchase it in advance and wear it to every fitting.

Try on a few different bras with your gown before you make your final decision. The most versatile style has removable straps, letting you create a crisscross back, halter, or strapless look. For a backless gown, you'll need a backless bra that hooks at the waist. For a strapless gown, wear a strapless bra or a set of flesh-colored cups that stick to your skin.

Many brides wear a corset-like bustier which has garters attached for stockings.

If you want to look a little slimmer on your wedding day, try an undergarment made with Lycra or Spandex.

When choosing the panties that you will wear under your wedding gown, again, go for comfort. If your gown has an unusually slinky cut or is made of very thin material, wear pantyhose with built-in underwear.

If your wedding gown requires that you wear a crinoline, your bridal shop will help you make the right choice. Often, crinolines can be rented.

Some brides like to wear a garter belt and stockings. However, the pressure of the stockings can pull a garter belt downward, leading to wrinkling at the knees and ankles. That's why many brides prefer silky pantyhose. Buy an extra pair in case you get a run.

Altering a Gown

If you want to wear your mother's wedding gown, or if you have fallen in love with a vintage gown, chances are it may need to be altered. Alterations can be anything from a few tucks to make the gown fit perfectly, to a complete makeover.

When choosing a seamstress to alter a wedding gown, hire someone who specializes in wedding attire. Ask to see their work, and be sure to check references carefully.

Before signing anything or handing over a deposit, get the important facts in writing. The work should be described in as much detail as possible, including the cost and the completion date.

Taking Measurements

You may be asked to provide your measurements over the phone. To ensure that you will be as accurate as possible, wear the lingerie that you will be wearing with your wedding gown. Stand straight, with your arms at your side.

Take your bust measurement across the widest part of your back. Do not use your bra size as your measurement.

The smallest part of your waist is your true waistline. Do not pull in your stomach, and leave room so that one finger can fit under the measuring tape.

When measuring your hips, measure at the fullest part.

To get an accurate hollow-to-hem measurement, wear the crinoline and shoes that you will be wearing with your gown. You will need two measurements: from the hollow of your neck to your waist, and from the waist to the hem.

Fittings

Since your largest measurement will be used when ordering, the gown will need to be altered to make it fit you perfectly. Most wedding gowns require two fittings; some need more.

At the first fitting you will see the dress for the first time since you ordered it from a sample. Be sure there are no defects in the buttons, stitching, or zipper. When you put it on, the seamstress will examine where it needs to be altered. Wear the shoes and lingerie that you will be wearing with the gown.

At the second fitting, try on the gown and examine it closely in a three-way mirror. Walk, turn, and move around to be sure the gown fits comfortably. If everything is fine, you won't need a third fitting.

Your third visit to the bridal boutique will probably be your last. Try the gown on once more, to be sure the alterations have been done satisfactorily, and make arrangements to pick it up just before the wedding. Bring your maid of honor to this fitting so she can learn how to bustle the train for dancing.

Bridesmaids, Maid of Honor, and Flower Girls

Bridesmaids no longer pay high prices for dresses they will only wear once. Today, there is a trend toward practicality. If possible, shop for the bridesmaids' dresses at a time when prom dresses are in the stores. They are better style-wise, less expensive, and they will be worn again.

As the bride, you have the final say in the bridesmaids' and maid of honor's dresses. However, you must consider their input. In order to look their best in your wedding photographs, it is important that your bridesmaids feel their best.

Shop with your maid of honor and choose her gown first. She can help you narrow the bridesmaid's dresses down to three. The bridesmaids can then agree on the final decision. Buy all the dresses from the same shop, as this will often get you a discount. If one of the bridesmaids lives some distance from the bride, she can handle the shopping problem by making use of the national bridal magazines and by sending her measurements to the shop by fax or telephone. All of the bridesmaids' dresses should be ordered together to ensure the same dye lot.

The bridesmaids can wear short dresses if the bride is wearing a long gown, but not the other way around. All hemlines should be the same distance from the floor for uniformity in the photographs.

All bridesmaids set up their own fitting appointments. Neither the bride nor her wedding planner is responsible for reminding them.

The flower girl's dress is usually white or ivory; the satin sash can be the color of the bridesmaids' dresses. Be sure to include her mother in the shopping, as she will be paying for the dress.

Mothers of the Bride and Groom

The bride's mother picks out her dress first and informs the groom's mother so she can choose accordingly. This way, they don't look too much alike but they don't clash, either.

The mothers' dresses must be in accordance with the formality of the wedding and they must not be too close in color to those of the bridesmaids.

As soon as they have both chosen their dresses, the mothers can advise the florist of the color, so that the corsages can be ordered. Alternatively, a white or ivory corsage can be worn with any color dress.

Do not suggest that your mother or your fiancé's mother buy a dress just because it will look good in the wedding photos. This is an important day for both of them and they need to be themselves.

Gown Preservation

Many dry cleaners preserve wedding gowns. Ask the bridal boutique or former brides to refer you to one.

Some stains, such as champagne, show up later. Point out these areas to the cleaner, and check the gown yearly for new stains. Underarm shields and bra inserts must be removed, as they will also cause staining. The cleaner must test any beading or trims that have been glued on, as many types of glue dissolve during the cleaning process.

Those sealed boxes with cellophane windows are lovely to look at, but they let in light and prevent air from circulating. This causes discoloration, so they should be avoided. Instead, puff up the sleeves and bodice with acid-free tissue and place the gown in an acid-free box.

You may prefer to hang the gown in a cool, dark closet. Direct sunlight will cause yellowing. Place the gown on a padded hanger and wrap in a muslin sheet. Mothball fumes can be damaging. Never hang the gown in a plastic bag, as plastic will trap moisture. Always use the loops sewn inside the shoulder seams. That way, the weight of the gown will not damage the seams. If the dress is not equipped with loops, sew them in.

With a little special treatment and planning ahead, your daughter may someday be married in the same dress!

The Groom

The groom's attire dictates what the rest of the men will wear. If he does not own a tuxedo, chances are he will rent rather than investing in one. The second-time groom can take his cue from the formality of the wedding. There are no etiquette restrictions for grooms, as there are for brides. Here is a quick look at the formalwear available for today's best-dressed grooms:

Tuxedo: The tuxedo can be either single or double-breasted and is available in the colors which are in style at the time. Black is classic. The "tux" is worn with a pleated white shirt, bow tie, and cummerbund. This is what is meant if an invitation specifies "black tie."

Tails: Also known as "full dress." The jacket can be single or double-breasted. It is short at the front with long tails at the back. It is worn at the most formal weddings.

Cutaway or morning coat: This jacket has a front waist button and tapers from the waist to a long wide tail at the back. Gray is the most popular color. The matching trousers are striped. The ensemble is completed by a wing-collar shirt, ascot tie, and matching or coordinating vest. A "four-in-hand" tie may be substituted for the ascot. This is considered proper for a very formal day-time wedding.

Dinner jacket: This is a white or ivory jacket that is worn with formal black trousers, black bow tie, and cummerbund. Think of Humphrey Bogart in *Casablanca.* This look is worn year-round for formal and semiformal weddings in warmer climates, and during the summer months everywhere else.

White tie: This is the ultimate in elegance. The tailcoat has two long back tails, and is worn in white, gray, navy, or burgundy. A wing-collar shirt, vest, and matching tie complete the ensemble.

Black suit: If the wedding is to be informal, the groom will wear a black suit. Often, grooms wear a suit for a semiformal wedding, especially if it is to be a small wedding.

Lapel widths go in and out of fashion. At any given time they can be wide, narrow, or in between. These are the three most popular lapel styles:

Notched: A lapel that has a triangular notch.

V: A lapel that meets the collar in a V-shape; the small notch points upward.

Shawl: A lapel with no notch; it smoothly flows from the neck to the buttons.

The Other Men in Your Life

The men in the wedding party (best man, ushers, fathers of the bride and groom, and ring bearer) will take their cue from the groom. Under no circumstances should the other men in the wedding party be dressed more formally than the groom. If he is wearing a tuxedo, they will too, although a suit would be appropriate for the fathers. All cities have formalwear rental stores with a large selection and full-color catalogues.

Unless their tuxedos include a vest, the best man and ushers wear cummerbunds to match their bow ties. These are available in many colors and often match the bridesmaids, with the best man matching the maid of honor.

If the groom is wearing a cutaway, the best man and ushers will wear strollers, which are longer than suit jackets but do not have tails.

The ring bearer would look very cute in a tuxedo, also available for rent. Or, he can wear a suit.

For an informal wedding, all men wear suits. If the groom chooses a suit for a small semiformal wedding, the others will wear suits.

If they will be wearing tuxedos, the shoes for all the men will be patent leather. These can also be rented.

Those who enjoy trivia will be interested to know that the tuxedo was named after Tuxedo Park, New York. Every year, a glittering ball was held there, the biggest social event of the year. In 1886, Griswold Lorillard, part of the circle known as the cream of New York society, designed for himself a short jacket with silk lapels. The tuxedo was born!

Wedding Gown Timeline

Nine to twelve months before the wedding:

- Define your tastes by cutting pictures out of wedding magazines
- Calculate your budget
- Ask other brides for the names of good bridal boutiques in your area
- Visit bridal boutiques and try on dresses that appeal to you
- Narrow down your choices
- Order the gown

Six to eight months before the wedding:

- Order the veil
- Confirm delivery date

Three to five months before the wedding

- Shop for bridesmaids' dresses
- Order lingerie, shoes, and accessories

Six weeks before the wedding

- Have the first fitting

Four weeks before the wedding

- Have the second fitting

Three weeks before the wedding

- Have a third fitting, if necessary

Two weeks before the wedding

- Pick up gown from the bridal boutique
- Pick up veil, shoes, and accessories

Two days before the wedding

- Steam or press the gown and have it hang until you are ready to get dressed

Wedding Gown and Accessories Worksheet

WEDDING GOWN

Bridal Boutique

Address
Telephone
Email
Hours
Salesperson

Manufacturer

Style number
Fabric
Color
Size

Measurements

Bust
Waist
Hips
Height

Date Ordered

Cost
Deposit
Balance due
Delivery or pick-up details

Fittings

Date
Time

Date
Time

Date
Time

VEIL OR HEADPIECE

Store

Address
Telephone
Email
Salesperson

Manufacturer

Style number

Date ordered

Cost
Deposit
Balance due
Delivery or pick-up details

SHOES

Store

Address
Telephone
Email

Hours
Salesperson

Manufacturer

Style number
Color
Size

Date Ordered

Cost
Deposit
Balance due
Delivery or pick-up details

GLOVES

Store

Address
Telephone
Email
Salesperson

Manufacturer

Style number
Color

Date Ordered

Cost
Deposit
Balance due
Delivery or pick-up details

Maid of Honor's Worksheet

Name
Telephone
Email

NAME OF BRIDAL BOUTIQUE

Telephone
Salesperson

GOWN

Style #
Manufacturer
Size
Fabric
Color

MEASUREMENTS

Bust
Waist
Hips
Height

DATE ORDERED

Cost
Deposit
Balance due
Delivery or pick-up details

FITTINGS

Date
Time

Date
Time

Date
Time

SHOES

Style #
Size
Color

GLOVES

Style
Size
Color

Bridesmaids' Worksheet

Name
Telephone
Email

NAME OF BRIDAL BOUTIQUE

Telephone
Salesperson

GOWN

Style #
Manufacturer
Size
Fabric
Color

MEASUREMENTS

Bust
Waist
Hips
Height

DATE ORDERED

Cost
Deposit
Balance due
Delivery or pick-up details

FITTINGS

Date
Time

Date
Time

Date
Time

SHOES

Style #
Size
Color

GLOVES

Style
Size
Color

Flower Girl's Worksheet

Name
Telephone
Email

NAME OF BRIDAL BOUTIQUE

Telephone
Salesperson

GOWN

Style #
Manufacturer
Size
Fabric
Color

DATE ORDERED

Cost
Deposit
Balance due
Delivery or pick-up details

FITTING

Date
Time

SHOES

Style #
Size
Color

GLOVES

Style
Size
Color

Groom's Formalwear Worksheet

RENTAL

Name
Telephone
Contact

TUXEDO

Manufacturer
Style #
Fabric
Color
Size

Measurements:

Chest
Waist
Hips
Height
Neck
Sleeve
Inseam

Ordered (date)
Fitting
Pick-up date
Return date

SHOES

Style#
Size
Color

BOW TIE

Style#
Color

CUMMERBUND

Style #
Color

VEST

Style #
Color
Size

SUSPENDERS

CUFFLINKS

Best Man's Formalwear Worksheet

RENTAL

Name
Telephone
Contact

TUXEDO

Manufacturer
Style #
Fabric
Color
Size
Measurements:
Chest
Waist
Hips
Height
Neck
Sleeve
Inseam
Ordered (date)
Fitting
Pick-up date
Return date

SHOES

Style#
Size
Color

BOW TIE

Style#
Color

CUMMERBUND

Style #
Color

VEST

Style #
Color
Size

SUSPENDERS

CUFFLINKS

Groomsman's Formalwear Worksheet

RENTAL

Name
Telephone
Contact

TUXEDO

Manufacturer
Style #
Fabric
Color
Size

Measurements:

Chest
Waist
Hips
Height
Neck
Sleeve
Inseam

Ordered (date)
Fitting
Pick-up date
Return date

SHOES

Style#
Size
Color

BOW TIE

Style#
Color

CUMMERBUND

Style #
Color

VEST

Style #
Color
Size

SUSPENDERS

CUFFLINKS

Ring Bearer's Formalwear Worksheet

RENTAL

Name
Telephone
Contact

TUXEDO

Manufacturer
Style #
Fabric
Color
Size
Measurements:
Chest
Waist
Hips
Height
Neck
Sleeve
Inseam
Ordered (date)
Fitting
Pick-up date
Return date

SHOES

Style#
Size
Color

BOW TIE

Style#
Color

CUMMERBUND

Style #
Color

VEST

Style #
Color
Size

Jewelry Worksheet

Store

Store
Salesperson
Address
Telephone
Hours

Engagement Ring

Description
Size
Price
Deposit
Balance due

Bride's Wedding Ring

Description
Size
Price
Deposit
Balance due

Groom's Wedding Ring

Description
Size
Price
Deposit
Balance due

Other Jewelry

Item 1: Description
Size
Price
Deposit
Balance due

Item 2: Description
Size
Price
Deposit
Balance due

Item 3: Description
Size
Price
Deposit
Balance due

For Your Notes

CHAPTER 4

Gifts And Guests

The Gift Registry

When choosing items to include in your gift registry, rely on your own tastes and the vision you have for the home you will share. Do your homework concerning quality and variety, and depend on the staff for general directions on the way the registry works.

The gift registry is a wonderful way to let friends and relatives know about your preferences. If you feel a little uncomfortable with the idea of "asking for gifts," remember that you will be doing your guests a favor. If you don't register, they will have to guess when choosing a gift and run the risk of choosing something that is not suitable. If you were a guest, wouldn't you be glad if the couple used a registry?

So how does it work? A wedding guest contacts the registry and can access all the items the couple has registered for, including the prices. Some registries will wrap the gift and deliver it directly to your home, or to the guest's home so that it can be presented in person.

Don't be too shy to register for some of the more expensive items; often, several friends decide go together on a larger gift. Choose smaller items as well, since many of your friends will use the registry for shower gifts. As well as the usual tableware and kitchen appliances, you can register for such items as luggage, cameras, and stereo equipment.

One large department store and two smaller stores will be more than enough. Gift registries are computerized and will immediately delete an item from the list when it has been purchased. This will cut down considerably on duplications. If you receive a registered gift that was purchased at another store, it only takes a telephone call to update the list. The greatest time saver of all is that the registry will provide you with a computerized list of purchases so there will be less chance of errors when writing thank-you notes.

After the wedding, you can either close the registry or keep it open for other gift-giving occasions. In the event that you don't receive all the gifts you registered for, you can use wedding gift money to shop the registry yourself, often at a discount.

One final point that cannot be emphasized enough: gift registry information can be included with shower invitations and spread by word of mouth. However, under no circumstances is it to be included with the wedding invitations!

In Chapter 23, you will find a list of items to consider when setting up your new home. Use it to supplement the list you get from your bridal registry consultant. She is professionally trained to help you make the right choices. The consultant will steer you toward the perfect colors, patterns, and manufacturers.

Gifts to the Wedding Party

Not only do you and your groom receive gifts, you also give them. One of the highlights of the bachelor party and bridesmaid's lunch will be when the grateful bride and groom each present their gifts to their attendants.

Some brides give the maid of honor and bridesmaids the jewelry that they will wear with their gowns. Gifts to the bridesmaids are identical, although the maid of honor's can be different. Besides jewelry, consider some of these other ideas:

- Lipstick case
- Silver spoon engraved with the wedding date
- Brass or silver picture fame
- Small jewelry case
- Music box

Gifts from the groom to his ushers will be identical, while the best man's can be different. Some ideas:

- Leather wallet
- Pen and pencil set
- Cuff links
- Tie clip
- Desk accessories in leather or silver

Don't forget the flower girl and ring bearer. A stuffed teddy bear with your names and wedding date is sure to delight them.

Recording Gifts

Wedding gifts must be recorded as they are opened to ensure that the thank-you notes are sent to the correct person and that none are overlooked. Remember these three rules:

- Record each gift as soon as it is opened.
- Do not have too many people opening and recording, as items can be more easily overlooked this way.
- Have a back-up system, which means that gifts are actually recorded twice.

The three main methods of recording gifts are the book, the cards, and the guest list. Use the book as the primary method, and either the guest list or cards as the backup. A computer file may take the place of an actual book.

Book: A specially-printed gift book can be purchased in any stationery or card store. You can also use a computer file or 3x5 index cards. Either way, each gift must be recorded immediately upon opening. Note the name and address of the sender, the store at which it was purchased, a description of the gift, the date the gift was received, and the date a thank-you note was sent. Many gift books come with numbered stickers. The gift will be recorded beside a number in the book; the corresponding sticker will be placed on the card that was enclosed with the gift.

Cards: If book stickers are used, the cards that were enclosed with the gifts will form a back-up system for recording the gifts. If you wish to use this system but do not have the stickers, print the same information of the back of the card as you did in the book. File them in a shoebox, in numerical order.

Guest list: Whether the guest list is an index card file, computer file, or binder, you will be able to use it to back-up your gift record. As you open each gift, locate the guest in your system, describe the gift (beside the gift make a note of when it was received), and the date a thank-you note was sent.

Thank-You Notes

No matter how large the wedding, it is not proper for thank-you notes to be delayed longer than three months. To avoid getting behind, sit down each day and write the notes for all of the gifts that arrived that day. Traditionally, these notes were written by the bride, although many couples do them together. Printed cards must *always* be accompanied by a personal note. A handwritten note on quality paper is also proper.

If an extended honeymoon will delay the writing of thank-you notes past three months, a printed card may be sent that states:

(Bride's Name)
acknowledges with thanks
the receipt of your wedding gift
and will write a personal note of appreciation at an early date.

This will let the giver know that the gift was received, but it is not a substitute for a proper thank-you note when you return home.

As you write your notes, refer to the gift specifically. "Thank you for the lovely wedding gift" is incorrect. Instead, say "Thank you for the lovely wine glasses." If you are not sure exactly what the gift is, try something like "the beautiful piece of sculpture." Money should be referred to as a "generous gift."

If a gift has arrived broken, contact the store for a replacement. The giver need never know. You should exchange a gift only if the giver will never find out or if identical gifts are received, in order to avoid hurt feelings.

Many couples write their thank-you notes on cards that feature their wedding picture. The only drawback is that the photographs must be back from the photographer before the cards can be sent. To speed up the process, pick up the envelopes from the photographer in advance. They can be addressed and ready to mail immediately when the cards are added. Refer back to your guest list; it has all the addresses!

Managing the Guest List

Start the guest list about nine months before the wedding. It can be done by computer or by using the guest list at the end this chapter.

Traditionally, the number of guests is estimated and both families take half. Or, one-quarter of the guest list goes to the bride, her family, the groom, and his family.

When the lists are combined there will be some duplication of mutual friends. This creates an opening for someone who wasn't included on the first list. Unused space on one side can be used to accommodate guests from the other side.

On the other hand, you may have more friends and family than space and budget permit. Invite a few extra people, as not everyone who receives your invitation will be able to attend. This is especially true if they live far away. Or, enlarge the guest list and make adjustments elsewhere. Again, your priorities will guide you.

Anyone who is married, engaged, or living with someone should not be invited singly. Find out the first name of their significant other if you don't already know the person. If your parents are divorced and remarried, you must also include their new spouses.

Should you send a wedding invitation to someone who is in mourning? This is a very difficult question. A wedding may be difficult for someone who has just lost a spouse. On the other hand, being with other people is good medicine. Send the invitation anyway–it is up to the recipient to accept or decline.

A wedding is not a social obligation. You should only invite those with whom you wish to share your special day.

Save-the-Date Cards

Save-the-date cards are a relatively new addition to the world of wedding stationery. These cards are used to provide guests with advance notice of your upcoming wedding in order to ensure that they will be able to attend. They are handy when you are planning a wedding for a popular long weekend and are concerned that guests will make other plans before receiving your invitation.

Send save-the-date cards three to six months prior to the wedding. If you send them any earlier than that, you run the risk of guests forgetting.

Purchase save-the-date cards through any wedding stationery dealer, mail order catalog, or printing company. Often, they are available in a style that will match your wedding invitations.

Save-the-date cards are not a substitute for wedding invitations; you still need to send those once the wedding date draws a little nearer.

Inviting Children

Couples decide not to invite children to their wedding reception for many reasons. Perhaps they wish to cut costs. Or, maybe they want to avoid the problem of young children fussing and running around.

Regardless of your harmless intentions, some guests are likely to be offended, so think it over carefully. If cost is the only factor, investigate the possibilities of children's dinners for much less than you'll pay for the adults. If you are concerned that the children might misbehave, hire someone to look after them in another room if they become bored or wild.

It is not correct to handprint anything on the invitations, so the printer must add the words "Adult reception" to the invitations. "Adults only reception" is also permissible, but "No children" is not considered proper.

It should go without saying that the flower girl and ring bearer cannot be excluded from the reception; I once heard of a bride who expected the ring bearer's parents to take him home right after the ceremony. They did, and haven't spoken to her since!

Despite your efforts to have guests show up without their children, you may have someone disregard your request and bring them anyway. This is the height of poor manners, but there is nothing you can do at this point. Depending on the caterer, there may be a provision for extra food; if not, the parents will have to share their meal with the child. Under no circumstances should you allow anything to ruin your memories of the day. Let it go.

Extra Guests

Often, an invited guest will ask to bring other people. Parents might ask to bring their teenaged children, who will in turn ask if they can bring a guest.

Only the individuals named on the inner envelope are included in the invitation. If they are to bring someone, the inner envelope will include the words "and guest."

Telephone the guest involved and gently but firmly explain that there has been a misunderstanding. Tell them that you would love to have the extra person, but that the venue holds only so many people, or that you are unable to stretch the budget to accommodate anyone else.

Un-Inviting a Guest

Once a wedding invitation has been issued, it is inappropriate to retract it. This includes verbal invitations. Only in *very* extreme circumstances, such as if someone is likely to become violent at the wedding, would you ever consider such a thing.

Brides sometimes tell friends and family that they will be allowing children, later to send "adult only" invitations. Others promise a wedding invitation to everyone they know, only to discover that the reception venue cannot hold them all, or that the budget cannot stretch that far.

Be careful not to say anything until you are sure, and until the guest list is completed and revised.

A sample guest list follows on the next page. Make as many copies of this page as you need.

Guest List

Name
Address
Telephone
Date sent RSVP Number in party
Gift Thank you sent

Name
Address
Telephone
Date sent RSVP Number in party
Gift Thank you sent

Name
Address
Telephone
Date sent RSVP Number in party
Gift Thank you sent

Name
Address
Telephone
Date sent RSVP Number in party
Gift Thank you sent

Name
Address
Telephone
Date sent RSVP Number in party
Gift Thank you sent

Name
Address
Telephone
Date sent RSVP Number in party
Gift Thank you sent

Name
Address
Telephone
Date sent RSVP Number in party
Gift Thank you sent

Name
Address
Telephone
Date sent RSVP Number in party
Gift Thank you sent

Name
Address
Telephone
Date sent RSVP Number in party
Gift Thank you sent

Name
Address
Telephone
Date sent RSVP Number in party
Gift Thank you sent

Out of Town Guests

Name
Cell phone
Date of arrival
Hotel
Reservation number
Confirmed
Hotel telephone
Room number
Date of departure

Name
Cell phone
Date of arrival
Hotel
Reservation number
Confirmed
Hotel telephone
Room number
Date of departure

For Your Notes

CHAPTER 5

Invitations and Other Wedding Stationery

Types of Invitations

There are four main types of wedding invitations on the market today, categorized by the way they are printed or the appearance they present.

- **Engraved:** These are considered to be the ultimate in wedding stationery. The invitation is engraved using a copper plate into which the wording is cut. The plate is inked and stamped against the card stock. This takes a great amount of pressure, which causes an indentation on the back of the paper and a raised-letter effect on the front. Engraving creates a look that is beyond compare. The copper plate is delivered with the order and makes a lovely keepsake. Additional invitations can be printed off this same plate, avoiding extra costs. This is the most expensive type of printing, but it is certainly worth the money for the bride who wants only the best.
- **Thermography**: Thermography uses a technique of placing powder on wet ink and putting it into an oven to produce a raised lettering. This gives the effect of engraving, but at a much lower cost. It is generally agreed that the paper is more important than the printing, and exquisite invitations are produced by using thermography and a paper with a high cotton content.

- **Printed**: Printed invitations are featured in the same catalogues as thermography. Because of their lower cost, they are often the first choice. Until recently, printed invitations have been considered socially incorrect. This has changed, as many couples are opting to print their own invitations on their home computers. For very formal weddings, though, they are not to be used.
- **Contemporary**: These are anything but traditional; they are as unique as the bride who sends them. The paper colors, ink colors, borders, pictures, and embossing are truly beautiful. Many brides like to coordinate their wedding invitations with their wedding colors.

Unsuitable Invitations

Preprinted invitations, with spaces to fill in the names of the bride and groom, are in the poorest of taste, and should *never* be used.

Under no circumstances should you ever invite guests to your wedding via email or telephone. And *never* use computer-generated address labels on the envelopes!

Unconventional Invitations

Many couples want their wedding invitations to be unlike anything their friends have ever seen before!

Use your imagination; sometimes, invitations can be sent in the form of a DVD or CD. You can even send champagne bottles with a label that is actually a wedding invitation!

This is the perfect way to let your guests know that a fun, off-beat wedding is about to take place. However, a traditional, formal wedding requires a traditional, formal invitation.

Papers and Inks

The best paper on which to print wedding invitations is made from 100 percent cotton fiber. It has a much softer and smoother texture than wood fiber paper. Although contemporary invitations are printed on papers of every color and pattern, the most popular paper colors are the traditional white and ecru.

Plain paper is generally preferred for an invitation that will be printed in a script-style font. However, a "paneled" paper (one that has an embossed border) is used with print-style fonts, as these are usually tighter and need the panel to focus the eye on the text.

Usually, invitation papers are folded, with the printing on the outside.

It was once considered correct to use only black ink. Today, brides can choose from a beautiful array of colors. Although many brides match the invitation ink to their wedding colors, be sure to choose an ink to enhance the invitation.

Wording of Formal Invitations

Each line on the invitation has a specific purpose. The following is the standard form for all Protestant wedding invitations. There are slight variations for Catholic and Jewish invitations, which are included in this chapter.

Invitational line: This line specifies the names of those issuing the invitation, usually the bride's parents. "Mr." and "Mrs." are the only abbreviations that are allowed. "Doctor" and all other titles are spelled out. Etiquette experts disagree on the use of "Jr." or "junior." Let the length of the line guide you, but note that if the word is written out, the "j" is lower case, and if it is abbreviated, the "J" is capitalized. Nicknames are not appropriate and full names are always used, never initials. Roman numerals II and III for "second" and "third" may be used. Two invitational lines can be used if the bride's and groom's parents are issuing the invitations jointly (the bride's parents are on the top line) or if divorced parents are issuing the invitation (the mother is on the top line). Until quite recently, this was frowned upon by etiquette experts, who insisted that the names of divorced parents should never appear on the invitation together. This is a good example of how times are changing; nevertheless, they are not to appear on the same line. Note that in these cases, the two lines are not joined by the word "and."

Request lines: The first of these lines indicates that the wedding will take place in a house of worship by using the wording "the honour of your presence." The English spelling of "honour" is always used. "The pleasure of your company" is used if the ceremony will take place at another location. The second request line will read "at the marriage of their daughter" unless the invitation is issued by someone other than the bride's parents. In this case it will indicate the issuer's relationship to the bride.

Bride's name: If both parents have the same last name, and if the bride's last name is the same as her parents, only her first and middle names will be used. Otherwise, her last name will be added. If the bride uses a professional title, her last name will be used.

Joining line: The word "to" is used to join the names of the bride and groom, except for Jewish invitations in which both sets of parents are listed at the top. In this case "and" is used.

Groom's name: The groom's first, middle and last names are used, as well as Mr., or any military or professional title he may hold. If the groom's parents are issuing the invitations, the bride's and groom's names remain in the same positions; the bride's last name is included. In this case, she is often addressed as "Miss."

Day and month: These can be preceded by the word "on," although it is not necessary. The date is written out in full with no abbreviation or numerals.

Year: The numbers of the year are spelled out, either capitalized or in lower case (but be consistent).

Time: The numbers are written out in lower case. The words "in the morning," "in the afternoon," or "in the evening" are optional. Quarter hours are not used. Half hours are indicated by "half after," not "half past." AM and PM are not used.

Location: The name of the church, synagogue, or other location. For a home wedding, this line is not used. The word "Saint" is usually spelled out, unless "St." is the form used in the name of the church.

Address: For a church or synagogue, this line is optional. For all other locations, and especially for a home wedding, include the street address. Numerals are used here unless the number is very short. For example, "Two" is spelled out. There is no comma after this line.

City, State, Province: The province or state is optional; if used, it is separated from the city by a comma.

Extra lines: Some etiquette experts disapprove of these lines, which are set to the left or the right. However, they do have their uses, most commonly for an RSVP to a home wedding. In this case, it will appear on two lines at the lower left. The first line is for "RSVP" and the second for the address, if different than that in the body of the invitation. The extra lines are also used to indicate "Best wishes only" when no gifts are requested. Be sure to determine if they add to the printing costs; they usually do.

RSVP: RSVP is an abbreviation for the French "repondez s'il vous plait." It is also appropriate to use "Please reply" or "A favour of a reply is requested." Again, note the English spelling of the word "favour."

Formal Invitation Spacing

Invitational line
Request line
Request line
Bride's name
Joining line
Groom's name
Day and month
Year
Time
Location
Address
City, state, or province

Extra lines (optional)

Standard Wording for Wedding Invitations

Example 1

Standard wording for a wedding held in a church

Mr. and Mrs. George Alexander Aldridge
request the honour of your presence
at the marriage of their daughter
Laura Michelle
to
Mr. William David Taunton
on Saturday, the tenth of June
two thousand and (year)
at one o'clock in the afternoon
Saint George's Anglican Church
Toronto, Ontario

Example 2

Standard wording for a wedding to be held in a location other than a church

Mr. and Mrs. George Alexander Aldridge
request the pleasure of your company
at the marriage of their daughter
Laura Michelle
to
Mr. William David Taunton
on Saturday, the tenth of June
two thousand and (year)
at one o'clock in the afternoon
Beaumark Golf and Country Club
Toronto, Ontario

Example 3

Standard wording if the bride's parents are divorced, the mother is remarried, and is issuing invitations with her new husband

Mr. and Mrs. Thomas Samuel Grant
request the honour of your presence
at the marriage of her daughter
Laura Michelle Aldridge
to
Mr. William David Taunton
on Saturday, the tenth of June
two thousand and (year)
at one o'clock in the afternoon
Saint George's Anglican Church
Toronto, Ontario

Example 4

Standard wording if the bride's parents are divorced, the bride's mother has not remarried and is issuing the invitations on her own

Anne Taylor Aldridge
(her maiden and married surnames) OR
Anne Marie Taylor
(if she resumes using her maiden name)
requests the honour of your presence
at the marriage of her daughter
Laura Michelle (Aldridge)
(use bride's surname only if it is different than her mother's)
to
Mr. William David Taunton
on Saturday, the tenth of June
two thousand and (year)
at one o'clock in the afternoon
Saint George's Anglican Church
Toronto, Ontario

Example 5

Standard wording if the bride's father is deceased, her mother has not remarried and is issuing the invitations on her own

Mrs. George Alexander Aldridge
(a widow uses her husband's name)
requests the honour of your presence
at the marriage of her daughter
Laura Michelle
to
Mr. William David Taunton
on Saturday, the tenth of June
two thousand and (year)
at one o'clock in the afternoon
Saint George's Anglican Church
Toronto, Ontario

Example 6

Standard wording if the bride's parents are divorced, neither remarried, and are hosting the wedding jointly

Mrs. Anne Aldridge
Mr. George Alexander Aldridge
request the honour of your presence
at the marriage of their daughter
Laura Michelle
to
Mr. William David Taunton
on Saturday, the tenth of June
two thousand and (year)
at one o'clock in the afternoon
Saint George's Anglican Church
Toronto, Ontario

Example 7

Standard wording if the bride's parents are divorced, both remarried, and are hosting the wedding jointly

Mrs. Thomas Samuel Grant
Mr. George Alexander Aldridge
request the honour of your presence
at the marriage of their daughter
Laura Michelle Aldridge
to
Mr. William David Taunton
on Saturday, the tenth of June
two thousand and (year)
at one o'clock in the afternoon
Saint George's Anglican Church
Toronto, Ontario

Note: Strictly speaking, their new spouses are not mentioned on the invitation, but the use of "Mr. and Mrs." is also acceptable.

Example 8

Standard wording if the bride's and groom's parents are hosting the wedding jointly

Mr. and Mrs. George Alexander Aldridge
Mr. and Mrs. James Edward Taunton
request the honour of your presence
at the marriage of
Miss Laura Michelle Aldridge
to
Mr. William David Taunton
on Saturday, the tenth of June
two thousand and (year)
at one o'clock in the afternoon
Saint George's Anglican Church
Toronto, Ontario

Example 9

Standard wording if the groom's parents are hosting the wedding

Mr. and Mrs. James Edward Taunton
request the honour of your presence
at the marriage of
Miss Laura Michelle Aldridgc
to their son
Mr. William David Taunton
on Saturday, the tenth of June
two thousand and (year)
at one o'clock in the afternoon
Saint George's Anglican Church
Toronto, Ontario

Example 10

Standard wording if the bride and groom are hosting their own wedding

Miss Laura Michelle Aldridge
and
Mr. William David Taunton
request the honour of your presence
at their marriage
Saturday, the tenth of June
two thousand and (year)
at one o'clock in the afternoon
Saint George's Anglican Church
Toronto, Ontario

Example 11

Alternate wording if the bride and groom are hosting their own wedding

The honour of your presence is requested
at the marriage of
Miss Laura Michelle Aldridge
to
Mr. William David Taunton
on Saturday, the tenth of June
two thousand and (year)
at one o'clock in the afternoon
Saint George's Anglican Church
Toronto, Ontario

Example 12

Standard wording if a relative is hosting the wedding

Mr. and Mrs. Henry Edward Spencer
request the honour of your presence
at the marriage of Mrs. Spencer's niece
Laura Michelle Aldridge
to
Mr. William David Taunton
on Saturday, the tenth of June
two thousand and (year)
at one o'clock in the afternoon
Saint George's Anglican Church
Toronto, Ontario

Example 13

Standard wording of a Jewish wedding invitation with both sets of parents at top

Mr. and Mrs. David Paul Goldstein
Mr. and Mrs. Jordan Samuel Black
request the honour of your presence
at the marriage of their children
Ruth Judith Goldstein
and
Nathan Abram Black
Thursday, the tenth of June
two thousand and (year)
at seven o'clock in the evening
Temple Beth Israel
Toronto, Ontario

Example 14

Standard wording of a Jewish wedding invitation with the groom's parents following

Mr. and Mrs. David Paul Goldstein
request the honour of your presence
at the marriage of their daughter
Ruth Judith
and
Mr. Nathan Abram Black
son of
Mr. and Mrs. Jordan Samuel Black
On Thursday, the tenth of June
two thousand and (year)
at seven o'clock in the evening
Temple Beth Israel
Toronto, Ontario

Example 15

Standard wording of a Catholic wedding invitation

Mr. and Mrs. George Alexander Aldridge
request the honour of your presence
at the Nuptial Mass at which their daughter
Laura Michelle
and
Mr. William David Taunton
will be united in the
Sacrament of Holy Matrimony
on Saturday, the tenth of June
two thousand and (year)
at twelve o'clock noon
Saint Michael's Cathedral
Toronto, Ontario

Example 16

Alternative wording for a Catholic wedding invitation

Mr. and Mrs. George Alexander Aldridge
request the honour of your presence
at the Wedding Mass at which their daughter
Laura Michelle
and
Mr. William David Taunton
will be united in the Sacrament of Marriage
on Saturday, the tenth of June
two thousand and (year)
at eleven o'clock in the morning
Saint Michael's Cathedral
Toronto, Ontario

Wording for Contemporary Invitations

Contemporary wedding invitations have many modern expressions, but they do not depart from the forms of proper etiquette. They include all of the pertinent information, and allow extra sentences at the beginning or at the end. This allows you to truly express your feelings about this most special day. Some common examples of contemporary wording are:

- Join us in the celebration of our love
- Our joy will be more complete if we can share it with you
- Witness our vows, as we become one in Christ
- Share with us the first day of our new life together
- Share in the blessings of our special day
- Our families invite you to become part of our happiness
- Come and worship with us

Reception Cards and Reception Invitations

The reception card is a smaller card, enclosed with the invitation. If only a handful of guests will be invited to a small reception, the bride's mother may send a handwritten note. It is not enclosed in the invitation.

If a very private ceremony is to be followed by a larger reception to which many guests will be invited, a reception invitation will be sent. It will resemble a wedding invitation in form and wording, with two exceptions: "at the marriage of their daughter" will be replaced by "at the wedding reception of their daughter," and the bride and groom will be joined by the word "and" instead of "to."

The reception card or the reception invitation will use the same paper, ink color, and font as the wedding invitation.

If all of the invited ceremony guests will also be invited to the reception, the reception information is often included in the left corner of the invitation. Strictly speaking, though, this is not considered proper, and the use of a small reception card is in order.

In any case, you must give the guests the required information, such as the time and place of the reception. "Immediately following the ceremony" is commonly used. Use terms such as "cocktail reception" or "dinner reception," so that your guests will know what to expect.

Wording examples of the reception card and the reception invitation follow on the next pages. The reception invitation is parallel to that of the wedding invitation.

Standard Wording of Reception Cards

The most common wording:

Reception following the ceremony
Rosehill Golf and Country Club
Toronto, Ontario
A favour of a reply is requested

Alternate wording of a reception card:

Reception and dinner half after eight o'clock
Rosehill Golf and Country Club
RSVP

Standard Wording of Reception Invitations

Example 1

The most common wording:

Mr. and Mrs. George Alexander Aldridge
request the pleasure of your company
at the wedding reception of their daughter
Laura Michelle
and
Mr. William David Taunton
on Saturday, the tenth of June
two thousand and (year)
at seven o'clock in the evening
Rosehill Golf and Country Club
Toronto, Ontario

Example 2

Standard wording if the bride's parents are divorced, the mother is remarried, and is issuing reception invitations with her new husband

Mr. and Mrs. Thomas Samuel Grant
request the pleasure of your company
at the wedding reception of her daughter
Laura Michelle
and
Mr. William David Taunton
on Saturday, the tenth of June
two thousand and (year)
at seven o'clock in the evening
Rosehill Golf and Country Club
Toronto, Ontario

Example 3

Standard wording if the bride's parents are divorced, the mother has not remarried, and is issuing the reception invitations on her own

Anne Taylor Aldridge
(her maiden and married surnames) OR
Anne Marie Taylor
(if she resumes using her maiden name)
requests the pleasure of your company
at the wedding reception of her daughter
Laura Michelle
and
Mr. William David Taunton
on Saturday, the tenth of June
two thousand and (year)
at seven o'clock in the evening
Rosehill Golf and Country Club
Toronto, Ontario

Example 4

Standard wording if the bride's parents are divorced, neither remarried, and are hosting the reception jointly

Mrs. Anne Aldridge
Mr. George Alexander Aldridge
request the pleasure of your company
at the wedding reception of their daughter
Laura Michelle
and
Mr. William David Taunton
on Saturday, the tenth of June
two thousand and (year)
at seven o'clock in the evening
Rosehill Golf and Country Club
Toronto, Ontario

Example 5

Standard wording if the bride's parents are divorced, both remarried, and are hosting the reception jointly

Mrs. Thomas Samuel Grant
Mr. George Alexander Aldridge
request the pleasure of your company
at the wedding reception of their daughter
Laura Michelle Aldridge
and
Mr. William David Taunton
on Saturday, the tenth of June
two thousand and (year)
at seven o'clock in the evening
Rosehill Golf and Country Club
Toronto, Ontario

Example 6

Standard wording if the bride's father is deceased, the mother has not remarried, and is issuing the reception invitation on her own

Mrs. George Alexander Aldridge
(a widow uses her husband's name)
requests the pleasure of your company
at the wedding reception of her daughter
Laura Michelle
and
Mr. William David Taunton
on Saturday, the tenth of June
two thousand and (year)
at seven o'clock in the evening
Rosehill Golf and Country Club
Toronto, Ontario

Example 7

Standard wording if the bride's and groom's parents are hosting the reception jointly

Mr. and Mrs. George Alexander Aldridge
Mr. and Mrs. James Edward Taunton
request the pleasure of your company
at the wedding reception of
Miss Laura Michelle Aldridge
and
Mr. William David Taunton
on Saturday, the tenth of June
two thousand and (year)
at seven o'clock in the evening
Rosehill Golf and Country Club
Toronto, Ontario

Example 8

Standard wording if the groom's parents are hosting the reception

Mr. and Mrs. James Edward Taunton
request the pleasure of your company
at the wedding reception of
Miss Laura Michelle Aldridge
and their son
Mr. William David Taunton
on Saturday, the tenth of June
two thousand and (year)
at seven o'clock in the evening
Rosehill Golf and Country Club
Toronto, Ontario

Example 9

Standard wording if the bride and groom are hosting their own reception

Miss Laura Michelle Aldridge
and
Mr. William David Taunton
request the pleasure of your company
at their wedding reception
Saturday, the tenth of June
two thousand and (year)
at seven o'clock in the evening
Rosehill Golf and Country Club
Toronto, Ontario

Example 10

Standard wording if a relative is hosting the reception

Mr. and Mrs. Henry Edward Spencer
request the pleasure of your company
at the wedding reception of Mrs. Spencer's niece
Laura Michelle Aldridge
and
Mr. William David Taunton
on Saturday, the tenth of June
two thousand and (year)
at seven o'clock in the evening
Rosehill Golf and Country Club
Toronto, Ontario

Reply Cards

Strictly speaking, an invitation to a church wedding does not require a response. The response is needed in order to provide the caterers with a head count for the reception.

Reply cards are smaller than invitations, the smallest size allowed by the post office. They are printed on the same paper and in the same font and ink color as the invitation. When enclosed in the wedding invitation with a self-addressed stamped envelope, they are a convenient way for wedding guests to respond to the invitation.

There are several different ways of wording these cards; choose the one that is best suited to your own purposes. Include a date by which the response is needed in order to plan the reception with the caterer.

The first includes a line beginning with the letter "M." The guest completes the word Mr. and Mrs./Mr./Mrs./Miss/Ms, and their name. They will then check "accepts" or "regrets," as the case may be. If only one person will be attending, it is acceptable to indicate one accept and one regret.

An alternative to this format is a second line that reads "will_attend." Guests fill the blank with a "yes" or a "no."

The next choice is similar to the first, but also adds a choice of menu.

Finally we have a reply card that uses a line on which guests indicate the number attending. The invitation is intended only for those named on the envelope. If a couple is invited with their child, the child's name will appear under those of the parents.

Reply card envelopes are printed with the home address of the bride's parents, or whoever is hosting the wedding. This eliminates the task of having to self-address them by hand.

An Alternative to the Reply Card

Many wedding invitations offer an option of a matching postcard to use as a response card. You can also print your own post cards. Office supply stores sell blank postcard stock, which you can print on your computer. Many of these come in colors, and even different textures, so you're sure to get exactly the right postcard to match the ambiance of your wedding.

When the Wedding Must be Postponed

If the new wedding date has already been set, an announcement of the postponement can be made with a new invitation. The wording is as follows.

Mr. and Mrs. George Alexander Aldridge
announce that the wedding of their daughter
Laura Michelle
to
Mr. William David Taunton
has been postponed from Saturday the tenth of June
until Saturday, the twentieth of September
at one o'clock in the afternoon
Saint George's Anglican Church
Toronto

Announcements

Announcements are sent after the wedding to anyone who could not be invited due to distance or budget. They are also used to inform friends and relatives of a small ceremony to which no guests were invited, but they are not sent to anyone who attended the wedding.

As with invitations, announcements are usually issued by the parents of the bride, but they can also be issued by the couple or on rare occasions by another relative.

Announcements are often ordered at the same time as the invitations, and usually in the same paper, ink color, and font. The wording is the only difference.

The announcement must include the day and date of the wedding (including the year), but not the time. The location is also noted (either the city alone, or the name of the church followed by the city), but not the address.

Wording of Wedding Announcements

Example 1

Wording of a wedding announcement issued by the bride's parents

Mr. and Mrs. George Alexander Aldridge
have the honour of announcing
the marriage of their daughter
Laura Michelle
to
Mr. William David Taunton
on Saturday, the tenth of June
two thousand and (year)
Saint George's Anglican Church
Toronto, Ontario

Example 2

Standard wording if the bride's parents are divorced, the mother is remarried, and is issuing announcements with her new husband

Mr. and Mrs. Thomas Samuel Grant
have the honour of announcing
the marriage of her daughter
Laura Michelle Aldridge
to
Mr. William David Taunton
on Saturday, the tenth of June
two thousand and (year)
Saint George's Anglican Church
Toronto, Ontario

Example 3

Standard wording if the bride's parents are divorced, the mother has not remarried, and is issuing the announcements on her own

Anne Taylor Aldridge
(her maiden and married surnames) OR
Anne Marie Taylor
(if she resumes using her maiden name)
has the honour of announcing
the marriage of her daughter
Laura Michelle (Aldridge)
(use her surname only if it is different than her mother's)
to
Mr. William David Taunton
on Saturday, the tenth of June
two thousand and (year)
Saint George's Anglican Church
Toronto, Ontario

Example 4

Standard wording if the bride's father is deceased, the mother has not remarried, and is issuing the announcements on her own

Mrs. George Alexander Aldridge
(a widow uses her husband's name)
has the honour of announcing
the marriage of her daughter
Laura Michelle
to
Mr. William David Taunton
on Saturday, the tenth of June
two thousand and (year)
Saint George's Anglican Church
Toronto, Ontario

Example 5

Standard wording if the bride's parents are divorced, neither remarried, and are announcing the wedding jointly

Mrs. Anne Aldridge
Mr. George Alexander Aldridge
have the honour of announcing
the marriage of their daughter
Laura Michelle
to
Mr. William David Taunton
on Saturday, the tenth of June
two thousand and (year)
Saint George's Anglican Church
Toronto, Ontario

Example 6

Standard wording if the bride's parents are divorced, both remarried, and are announcing the wedding jointly

Mrs. Thomas Samuel Grant
Mr. George Alexander Aldridge
have the honour of announcing
the marriage of their daughter
Laura Michelle
to
Mr. William David Taunton
on Saturday, the tenth of June
two thousand and (year)
Saint George's Anglican Church
Toronto, Ontario

Note: It is also acceptable to include the new spouses by the use of "Mr. and Mrs."

Example 7

Standard wording if the bride's and groom's parents are announcing the wedding jointly

Please note that both sets of parents rarely make a joint announcement. Use this form only if circumstances require it.

Mr. and Mrs. George Alexander Aldridge
Mr. and Mrs. James Edward Taunton
have the honour of announcing
the marriage of
Miss Laura Michelle Aldridge
to
Mr. William David Taunton
on Saturday, the tenth of June
two thousand and (year)
Saint George's Anglican Church
Toronto, Ontario

Example 8

Standard wording if the groom's parents are announcing the wedding

Please note that the groom's parents formally announce their son's marriage only if the bride has no parents or family to do so.

Mr. and Mrs. James Edward Taunton
have the honour of announcing
the marriage of
Miss Laura Michelle Aldridge
to their son
Mr. William David Taunton
on Saturday, the tenth of June
two thousand and (year)
Saint George's Anglican Church
Toronto, Ontario

Example 9

Standard wording of a wedding announcement issued by the couple

Miss Laura Michelle Aldridge
and
Mr. William David Taunton
announce their marriage
on Saturday, the tenth of June
two thousand and (year)
Saint George's Anglican Church
Toronto, Ontario

Example 10

Alternative wording of a wedding announcement

The marriage of
Miss Laura Michelle Aldridge
and
Mr. William David Taunton
took place
on Saturday, the tenth of June
two thousand and (year)
Saint George's Anglican Church
Toronto, Ontario

Example 11

Standard wording if a relative is announcing the wedding

Mr. and Mrs. Henry Edward Spencer
have the honour of announcing
the marriage of Mrs. Spencer's niece
Laura Michelle Aldridge
to
Mr. William David Taunton
on Saturday, the tenth of June
two thousand and (year)
Saint George's Anglican Church
Toronto, Ontario

Pew Cards

Pew cards are optional. If a special guest is to be seated in the first few pews of the church, they will receive a small card known as a "pew card," which identifies the actual pew in which the guest is to be seated. Grandparents and siblings are automatically seated in the second pew, but cards are commonly sent to godparents or to the parents of the flower girl and ring bearer.

It is acceptable to send the pew cards with the invitations. However, it has become common practice to send the cards at a later date. This will give you an idea of who will be attending the wedding. The cards are then mailed to those who have accepted.

The paper, ink color, and font style of these cards matches those of the wedding invitation.

(hand-write the guest's name)
will present this card to an usher at
Saint Paul's Cathedral
Pew number (print pew number)

OR

Please present this card at
Saint Paul's Cathedral
Saturday, the tenth of June
(write by hand "Bride's reserved section"
or "Groom's reserved section")

Maps and Directions

Directions and maps are frequently included for guests who are unfamiliar with the church location. Couples often print these themselves on their home computers. Print it on a separate card, unfolded, in the same style as the invitation. The paper must be of good quality. It goes without saying that cheap photocopies are unacceptable!

Directions and maps to the reception are not included in the invitation. Have the ushers distribute reception directions to those who need them.

Admission Cards and Parking Passes

Admission cards are enclosed with the invitation if the wedding is to take place at a location to which admission is charged, for example, a destination wedding held at Walt Disney World in Orlando, Florida.

If your reception location charges for parking, it is customary to include a parking pass that the guest can display on their dashboard.

Related Items

Most wedding invitation catalogues feature add-on items. Although not actually stationery, they are placed in the same category for convenience and are often personalized with the names of the bride and groom and their wedding date, in the same font and color as the invitations. These include, but are not limited to:

- Napkins
- Matchbooks
- Programs
- Cake boxes
- Tags for favors

Addressing the Envelopes

Two envelopes are used for a formal wedding invitation. The inner envelope is often lined in a color complimenting the invitation. It has no other information but the name(s) of those included in the invitation, often written in calligraphy.

The outer envelope is addressed as any other mail, with street names spelled out and postal/zip codes included. Beautiful postage stamps will add a special touch. Remember to get stamps for the reply card envelopes as well.

The outer envelope has the return address engraved, embossed or thermographed on its flap. This will be done when the invitations are ordered. The outer envelope must be addressed by hand. Don't use your computer, even if your handwriting is not beautiful.

Street numbers are written as numerals, but streets with a number in their name, such as Fifth Avenue, are spelled out. Provinces, states, and countries are always spelled out, never abbreviated.

Each line of the address is indented from the one above it. Never use a comma at the end of a line; use it only to separate words within the line.

Spell out all names, never use initials, and be sure to use correct titles (again, spelled out in full).

On the outer envelope, use first names, such as "Mr. and Mrs. James Wilson Hicks," but on the inner envelope simply "Mr. and Mrs. Hicks." If they are intimate friends or relatives, use "Jim and Betty," "Uncle Jim and Aunt Betty," depending on the relationship.

Unmarried people living together should have their names on separate lines of the outer envelope like this:

Miss Jill Brown
Mr. William Richardson

On the inner envelope their names appear on the same line, for example, "Miss Brown and Mr. Richardson" (or "Jill and Bill" for friends and close relatives).

When addressing a wedding invitation to a woman with a professional title, whether or not the husband also has a title, her name should appear on the outer envelope on a line by itself, above her husband's name. Do not abbreviate "Doctor," or use the word "and" to separate the husband's and wife's names. For example:

Doctor Mary Smith
Mr. Robert Smith

If both the husband and wife are doctors, it would look like this:

Doctor Mary Smith

Doctor Robert Smith

"David and guest" is unacceptable. If David has a wife, girlfriend, or fiancé, her first name must appear on the invitation. The same goes for "Philip and Laura, and family." If children are invited, address the outer envelope to the parents only. The children's names will appear on the inner envelope beneath their parents' names. Everyone over the age of eighteen, even if they still live at home, must receive their own invitation. If two adults other than a couple share an address, each must receive a separate invitation.

Invitations are mailed approximately six weeks before the wedding. Many experts recommend four weeks, but some invitees may have already made other plans by the time the invitation arrives. Allow extra time if you will be sending an invitation internationally. Have the post office weigh the assembled envelope to be sure you will be using the correct amount of postage.

Members of the wedding party and close family members (including parents and siblings) will want invitations as keepsakes, and it is customary to mail them one. Don't forget invitations for the clergy and his/her spouse.

For help with unusual situations while addressing your wedding invitations, check your local library for a complete and up-to-date etiquette encyclopedia.

Assembling the Envelopes

The inner envelope, already addressed, will contain all or some of these:

- Invitation
- Reception card
- Response card and its envelope
- Map or directions to the church
- Pew card

If the invitation is printed on folded stock, fold it so that the printing is on the outside. The invitation will be on the bottom, printed side up. There is no rule regarding the order in which the various pieces are placed on the invitation. They are usually placed according to size, with the smallest on the top. Place the reply card under the flap of its envelope.

Alternatively, the enclosures can be placed inside the fold of the invitation. The stack of enclosures is inserted into the inner envelope folded side first.

The printed side should face the back of the envelope, so that guests will see it when they open the envelope. The inner envelope is not gummed; the flap is to remain untucked.

Place the inner envelope into the outer envelope (which has already been addressed), with the name of the recipient facing the back of the envelope. When the outer envelope is opened, your guest should see the front face of the inner envelope.

How Many Invitations Should be Ordered?

As a general rule, divide your guest list in half and add twenty-five. Using this formula, if you are inviting two hundred people, you will order one hundred and twenty-five invitations. You must make adjustments if your guest list consists of more single people than couples.

Not everyone who receives an invitation to your wedding will be able to attend. There is also a formula for estimating how many people you will actually have at the wedding: Double the number of invitations you sent and subtract one third. Round up if you get a fraction.

For the one hundred and twenty-five invitations you issued in the previous example, you can expect one hundred and sixty-eight guests to attend.

When you order your invitations, you will see that the bulk of the cost is for the first run. Depending on the printer, the first run will consist of fifty, seventy-five, or one hundred invitations. If the same order specifies higher quantities, you will find that each increment of twenty-five invitations costs very little. Therefore it is much more cost effective to order more than you will need. This will give you extras for keepsakes.

Stationery Worksheet

STATIONER

Address

Telephone

Fax

Contact person

Order date

Pick up date

Total Cost

Deposit

Balance due

INVITATIONS

Quantity

Style #

Paper

Font

Color

Return address for envelope

Attach wording on a separate sheet

REPLY CARDS

Quantity

Style #

Paper

Font

Color

Address for reply card envelopes

Attach wording on a separate sheet

RECEPTION CARDS

Quantity

Style #

Paper

Font

Color

Attach wording on a separate sheet

PEW CARDS

Quantity

Style #

Paper

Font

Color

Attach wording on a separate sheet

ANNOUNCEMENTS

Quantity

Style #

Paper

Font

Color

Attach wording on a separate sheet

Invitation Wording Worksheet

Invitational line:

Request line:

Request line:

Bride's name:

Joining line:

Groom's name:

Day and month:

Year:

Time:

Location:

Address:

City, state or province:

Extra lines (optional):

For Your Notes

CHAPTER 6

Wedding Flowers

Working with Your Florist

It is safe to assume that the florist's work will appear in every one of your wedding photographs. Before your first appointment, gather photographs of the church and reception site, and photographs/swatches of your gown and bridesmaids' dresses. The more detail you can provide, the happier you will be with the finished result.

Inside her shop, the florist will have silk replicas of her bouquets, or she will be able to show you pictures. Tell her your ideas for both the ceremony and the reception; listen to her suggestions. Discuss the flowers you simply must have; she will recommend ways to show them off at their best.

Personal flowers will be delivered to your home on the morning of the wedding, and other flowers to the church or to the reception location.

You will find a "Floral Worksheet" at the end of this chapter. Use it to determine the flowers you need to order.

The Elements of Design as They Relate to Wedding Flowers

The elements of design are balance, scale, texture, rhythm, line, harmony, and color. These also apply to floral design, with an added element: scent.

These elements are generally conspicuous only when they are absent. Professionals will ensure that the wedding flowers are combined with these elements in mind, but they will often break the rules for the sake of artistic expression.

Color follows separately, as it is the most important.

Bouquets and floral compositions have a focal point, a feature that draws the eye into the arrangement. Harmony (also called unity) means that all of the flowers and greenery will blend together and be pleasing to the eye.

Line refers to the direction in which the eye moves when viewing the arrangement. Vertical lines will make it appear taller; horizontal lines will make it seem wider.

Texture is introduced by the use of different flowers and varieties of greenery. Rhythm is achieved by using certain flowers and greenery within the arrangement, in harmony with other arrangements used for the same wedding.

Balance, shape, and proportion go together to ensure that the bouquet or arrangement fits well into its surroundings, and is constructed in such a way that it will not appear top-heavy or odd-looking in any way.

Don't ignore scent; certain combinations are pleasing to the nose, whereas others are not.

The Use of Color in Wedding Flowers

The colors used in wedding flowers will determine, and be determined by, the colors used in the other components of the wedding.

A monochromatic color scheme is one that uses only one color in varying shades and tints, such as pink and rose.

The complimentary color scheme uses two colors that are opposites on the color wheel. Complimentary colors are:

- Red and green (try pink here)
- Yellow and violet (or lilac)
- Blue and orange (go for a nice peach color)

Color contrasts are those which are sometimes described as "clashing." While some of these are a little jarring in their pure forms, they can be used together as pastels. Examples are:

- Yellow and red
- Green and orange
- Red and blue
- Orange and violet
- Blue and yellow

You can also put together a complimentary and a contrasting pair. Imagine pale tints of peach, yellow and blue, combined with green foliage in a bouquet of wildflowers carried by a bridesmaid, and you'll get the idea.

Traditionally, the bride carried a bouquet of white, off-white, or cream flowers. Interest was added by varying the varieties of flowers. Since the all-white bouquet doesn't photograph too well against a white wedding gown, it has become common to add just a touch of color to the bride's bouquet. "Blush" is a non-color that will give the desired effect.

Some brides depart from the traditional bouquet, coordinating their bouquets to the color scheme of the wedding. Others choose flowers in contrasting colors. Do be aware, though, that adding brightly colored flowers randomly throughout a white bouquet creates an odd effect in photographs.

Silk vs Fresh

There are many advantages to using at least some silk in your wedding flowers. If you have your heart set on an exotic or out-of-season flower, silk will allow you to create the same effect without breaking the budget. Many floral designers use a combination of fresh and silk flowers. Some use silk exclusively.

The possibility of keeping the wedding bouquet forever is appealing to the sentimental nature of many brides. So is the idea of having floral arrangements in the home that were originally part of the wedding reception. Silk makes this possible.

In a very hot climate, it may be difficult to keep fresh flowers from wilting, a problem that you don't experience with silk flowers. Combine silk flowers with fresh greenery, and spray them with scent.

Finally, silk bouquets and boutonnieres are the perfect choice for any member of the wedding party who suffers from allergies.

That said, there is nothing like the look and scent of fresh flowers. Many brides prefer them, regardless of the advantages of silk.

Personal Flowers

"Personal flowers" are flowers that will be worn or carried by a person. They include:

- Bride's bouquet
- Bride's throwing bouquet
- Bride's going-away corsage
- Groom's boutonniere
- Bridesmaids' and maid of honor's bouquets
- Ushers' boutonnieres
- Flower girl's basket, filled with rose petals or with flowers
- Ring bearer's boutonniere
- Ring bearer's pillow, if it has flowers attached
- Corsages for the mothers of the bride and groom
- Boutonnieres for the fathers of the bride and groom
- Corsages and boutonnieres for the grandparents of the bride and groom
- Boutonnieres and corsages for readers, soloists, and anyone who will have a special part in the ceremony

The bride's bouquet is larger and more elaborate than that of the bridesmaids. Your choice will depend on the formality of your gown and your height. A tiny bride in a simple gown will be overwhelmed by a large cascade bouquet.

The groom's boutonniere should be somehow set apart as special; one way to do this is to include a flower from the bride's bouquet. The ushers' boutonnieres should be coordinated to the bridesmaids' bouquets.

Bouquet Styles

- **Crescent:** A bouquet is formed in a graceful curve
- **Nosegay:** A round bouquet, also known as "Colonial," or "posy"
- **Cascade:** A bouquet created with a fullness of flowers at the top, trailing to a cascade; roses are traditionally used and ivy will soften the look

- **Tussy-mussy**: A Victorian horn-shaped flower holder; a center flower is surrounded by smaller flowers, and then greenery
- **Spray bouquet:** This bouquet is known as the "free form" because loose flowers and greenery project from it at different angles
- **Hand-tied bouquet:** A more natural looking bouquet, with the stems of the flowers partially or entirely wrapped in ribbon

Alternatives to the Traditional Bouquet

- **Prayer book:** The bride can carry a prayer book decorated with flowers
- **Single flower:** Very dramatic, especially with a flower such as a calla lily
- **Fan:** A lace fan covered with flowers is especially lovely
- **Wreath:** Flower girls and bridesmaids can carry wreaths of flowers
- **Basket**: Although this is usually a style for the flower girl, it is traditionally a garden wedding style and can be carried by bridesmaids in such a wedding
- **Pomander:** A large ball of flowers with a wrist loop attached

Special Features of Bridal Bouquets

The bouquet can be made so that it allows for the presentation of roses to the mothers, the throwing bouquet, or the corsage you will wear as you leave for your honeymoon, but not all three.

As a touching gesture to the mothers, the bouquet can contain two detachable roses. The roses can be presented as you and your new husband are about to lead the recessional out of the church. Consider giving a rose to each other's mother. Face your guests (or give them a side view) as you detach the roses, so that they realize the flowers have come from your bouquet.

The bouquet can be designed in such a way that a small part of it (three flowers, some baby's breath, and ivy) can be removed, creating the throwing bouquet. The bouquet should be designed in such a way that the breakaway bouquet merely adds fullness. It should not be such an important part of the bouquet that it will destroy the look of the remaining arrangement when it is removed.

A detachable corsage can be built into the bouquet, which you can wear with your going-away outfit.

Do not remove and reinsert any of the detachable parts of the bouquet. To do so will affect the fit of the stem in the oasis, and the bouquet will detach before it is supposed to.

The Corsage

Regardless of the color scheme of the wedding, the mothers of the bride and groom wear corsages that compliment their own dresses. If the dresses will not be chosen until the last minute, an ivory or cream corsage can be ordered. It may be necessary to order a wrist corsage if a dress is of a particularly delicate fabric.

It is not necessary that any of the other corsages coordinate with the dresses of the wearers. Ivory or cream flowers will be appropriate for all. Grandmothers should have identical corsages to avoid the mistaken impression of favoritism. These ladies need corsages:

- Mother of the bride
- Mother of the groom
- Grandmother(s) of the bride
- Grandmother(s) of the groom
- Soloist
- Readers
- Organist

The Boutonniere

Boutonnieres are worn by the groom, best man, ushers, ring bearer, fathers, grandfathers, and any other honored man, such as a soloist.

Most often, the groom wears a flower from the bride's bouquet, and the ushers' boutonnieres coordinate with the bridesmaids' bouquets. It is necessary that all men in the wedding party wear a boutonniere in order to present a unified appearance. In the event that someone is allergic, a silk version of the same flower can be substituted.

Although the bride's and groom's families are each responsible for their own personal flowers, all boutonnieres and corsages should be ordered from the same florist.

Ceremony Flowers

Each church or ceremony location has its own special atmosphere; create a floral scheme that enhances that ambiance. There is no need to go overboard on flowers for the church, as each church is beautiful in its own right. Consider the size, style, and existing color scheme of the surroundings.

The altar flowers are usually the first to be chosen. These should be large and tall. Many brides place one standing arrangement on each side of the altar. Rented trees can be used to decorate the altar area.

If the church is large and the guest list is small, silk trees or topiaries can be used as dividers, creating the feeling of a cozier space in the front-most pews.

Wedding arches and chuppahs are yet another way to incorporate flowers into the ceremony. Both work well with floral garlands.

Reception Flowers

The flowers chosen to decorate the reception will create the mood and reinforce the color scheme. They include the following:

- Table centerpieces
- Floral garland for the head table
- Fresh or silk flowers on the wedding cake
- Topiaries or trees with twinkling lights
- Floral arrangements in special places, such as on a grand piano
- Flowers on a guest book table

- Flower rings to decorate the candelabra
- Bud vases with a single flower in the rest rooms
- Flower arrangements to decorate a buffet table
- Floral arrangement on the bar
- Flowers to decorate the cake knife

Items such as trees and topiaries can be rented from the florist. Use them to fill corners of the reception hall if the guest list is small.

If fresh flowers will be used on the cake, the florist will order non-toxic varieties on which no pesticides or chemicals have been used. A garland of greenery also looks great around the base of the cake.

Candelabra decorations usually consist of a ring of flowers or greenery at the base, perhaps trailing upward. Alternatively, a wreath of flowers can be nestled among the arms.

Many churches ask that flowers be removed after the ceremony. Couples on a budget can take them to decorate the reception. After the reception, the flowers can be given to a relative who was unable to attend, or donated to a local hospital or nursing home.

Unifying the Flowers

All of the bouquets and floral arrangements used in the wedding must relate to one another in order to present a unified appearance.

The flowers need not be identical, but they must harmonize. This requires a common element, such as flower type or flower color. The maid of honor's bouquet is usually different in some way than those of the bridesmaids in order to set her apart. Have the bouquet different in *one* aspect only, such as slightly larger or a slightly deeper color.

The bridesmaids carry smaller bouquets than the bride. If the flowers of the bride's bouquet contain pale pink, the bridesmaids' bouquets will be pink. This, in turn, will coordinate with the color of their dresses.

The floral arrangements must be unified with the setting in which they will be placed. For example, a rustic chapel in the country will be more suitable for wildflowers than for elaborate arrangements in crystal or silver containers. The size of the floral arrangements must be in scale to the room. Pew bows and chuppahs must be considered in the same manner.

A garden wedding will probably not need additional floral arrangements. When choosing bouquets, consider the colors of the flowers in the garden.

Popular Wedding Flowers

- Rose: Standard size and "sweetheart" roses come in many colors
- Baby's breath: Small, white, delicate flowers, often used as filler
- Carnation: Inexpensive, available year-round, and comes in a variety of colors. Often used with other flowers to stretch the budget
- Daffodil: Varieties of yellow to white
- Forget-me-not: Dainty blue flower with a yellow or white center
- Amaryllis: Deep red and white, shaped like a lily
- Bachelor button: Like tiny carnations, in pink, blue, white, or red
- Daisy: White with a yellow center
- Violet: Tiny white, blue, or purple flowers
- Gardenia: White flower with dark green leaves
- Lilac: Stalks of tiny white or lavender flowers
- Stephanotis: Small trumpet-shaped flowers on vines
- Iris: Large petals, two of which slightly droop, in white, yellow, blue, orange, or violet
- Delphinium: Long spikes of flowers in rose, blue, lavender, or white, with lacy foliage
- Tulip: Goblet-shaped flower in a variety of colors
- Aster: In pink, white, rose, or purple
- Freesia: Small flower in red, blue, orange, yellow, pink, lavender, or white

Varieties of Orchids

- Spray orchids: Tiny flowers on long spikes; available in winter but quite expensive
- Dendrobium: Miniature orchid; comes in sprays

- Japhet: Large; yellow throat; all-over curly edge
- Cymbidium: Smaller than Japhet; curly edge at center only
- Phalaenopsis: White with a reddish throat; round edge; not very durable
- Cattleya: Large; white with lavender or pink toward the center

Varieties of Lilies

- Calla: Large, long, white; thick stalks
- Stargazer: Large, star-shaped, protruding stamen; pink with white markings, or solid colors
- Day Lily: In shades of cream, yellow, red, or orange
- Alstroemeria: Miniature lilies in a variety of colors, or multicolor
- Lily of the valley: Small white clusters; bell-like
- Rubrum: Star-shaped; variety of colors

Varieties of Roses

- Bridal pink: Bright pink
- Lady Diana: Pale peach
- Diane de Poitiers: Deeper peach
- Darling: Creamy peach
- Sterling silver: Small, lavender
- Champagne: Creamy ivory
- Jacaranda: Hot pink
- Mademoiselle: Pink
- Jacqueline: Small, true red
- Delta Dawn: Medium yellow
- Silver angel: Mauve and mauve blend
- Camelot: Medium pink

The Language of Flowers

- Acacia: Friendship

- Agrimony: Gratitude
- Ambrosia: Love returned
- Anemone: Expectation
- Apple blossoms: Hope
- Lily of the valley: Happiness
- Azalea: Temperance
- Baby's breath: Innocence
- Bay laurel: Glory
- Calla lily: Beauty
- Carnation: Devotion
- Queen Anne's lace: Trust
- Chrysanthemum: Abundance
- Rosemary: Remembrance
- Forget-me-not: Remembrance
- Stephanotis: Marital happiness
- Tulip: Passion
- Violet: Modesty
- Ivy: Fidelity
- Larkspur: Laughter
- Laurel: Peace
- Lilac: Humility
- Lily: Majesty
- Aster: Elegance
- Myrtle: Remembrance
- Orange Blossom: Purity
- Orchid: Rare beauty
- Camellia: Loveliness
- Peony: Bashfulness
- Rose: Love
- Daffodil: Regard
- Daisy: Gentleness
- Freesia: Innocence
- Gardenia: Purity
- Heather: Future fortune
- Zinnia: Affection

Birth Month Flowers

- January: Carnation
- February: Violet
- March: Jonquil
- April: Sweet pea
- May: Lily of the valley
- June: Rose
- July: Larkspur
- August: Gladiolus
- September: Aster
- October: Calendula
- November: Chrysanthemum
- December: Narcissus

Flowers by Color

Pink:

- Amaryllis
- Camellia
- Carnation
- Freesia
- Gerbera daisy
- Peony
- Ranunculus
- Rose
- Tulip

White:

- Amaryllis
- Aster
- Baby's breath
- Calla lily
- Camellia
- Carnation
- Daisy
- Delphinium
- Freesia
- Gardenia
- Gladiolus
- Iris
- Lily of the valley
- Magnolia
- Peony
- Rose
- Stephanotis
- Tulip

Yellow:

- Chrysanthemum
- Daffodil
- Day lily
- Freesia
- Iris
- Rose
- Gerbera daisy
- Sunflower
- Tulip

Red:

- Amaryllis
- Camellia
- Carnation
- Freesia
- Rose
- Tulip

Blue:

- Anemone
- Delphinium
- Hyacinth
- Hydrangea
- Iris

Peach:

- Lily
- Gerbera daisy
- Tulip
- Rose

Purple:

- Aster
- Anemone
- Chrysanthemum
- Iris
- Gladiolus
- Orchid
- Delphinium
- Freesia

Orange:

- Day lily
- Gerbera daisy
- Rose
- Tulip

Flowers by Season

Spring:

- Apple blossom
- Cherry blossom
- Forsythia
- Larkspur
- Lily of the valley
- Sweet pea
- Daffodil
- Iris
- Lilac
- Lily
- Tulip
- Violet

Summer:

- Aster
- Dahlia
- Larkspur
- Calla lily
- Daisy
- Hydrangea
- Rose

Fall:

- Aster
- Chrysanthemum
- Shasta daisy
- Dahlia
- Marigold
- Zinnia

Year-Round: These are grown in greenhouses, and are available whatever the season.

- Baby's breath
- Bachelor button
- Delphinium
- Gardenia
- Rose
- Carnation
- Ivy
- Lily
- Orchid
- Stephanotis

Unwiltables

These flowers and their greenery will stand up throughout the wedding and reception.

- Baby's breath
- Bachelor button
- Delphinium
- Gardenia
- Carnation
- Daisy
- Ivy
- Lily
- Rose
- Orchid
- Stephanotis

Floral Preservation

After taking such care to choose your bouquet, and considering the sentimental nature of it, you will probably want to preserve it after the wedding.

The bouquet is preserved by one of several methods and displayed in a specially-made case. The process can take eight to twelve weeks. Visit the businesses in your area that perform this service. Not only must they be skilled in the actual preservation, but also in the composition of the arrangement. Floral designers are often hired for the job. To help you understand the process better, here are the four main methods:

- **Air-drying:** This is the least satisfactory of the four, as flowers often lose their color, shape, and size.
- **Pressing:** Flowers that have been pressed will last forever if they are kept under glass and treated for color enhancing. Remember, though, that they will be flattened.
- **Freeze-drying:** Effective, although flowers such as daisies and chrysanthemums cannot withstand the process.
- **Drying desiccants:** This method works by removing all moisture from the petals, and is the best of the four. Your flowers must be flawless, as brown spots cannot be preserved.

As an alternative to preservation, many brides dry their flowers and turn them into potpourri, which they display in crystal bowls.

Floral Worksheet

FLORIST

Name
Address
Telephone
Fax
Contact Person
Email

Delivery Instructions

Date of wedding
Ceremony location
Time of ceremony
Reception location
Time of reception

CEREMONY FLOWERS

Altar

Quantity
Flowers
Color
Cost

Pew Bows

Quantity
Flowers
Color
Cost

Windowsills

Quantity
Flowers
Color
Cost

Floral/Ivy garland

Quantity
Flowers
Color
Cost

Other

Quantity
Flowers
Color
Cost

TOTAL CEREMONY: $

PERSONAL FLOWERS

Bride

Flowers
Color
Cost

Maid of Honor

Flowers
Color
Cost

Bridesmaids

Quantity
Flowers
Color
Cost

Flower Girl

Details

Flowers

Color

Cost

Mothers

Quantity

Flowers

Color

Cost

Other corsages

Quantity

Flowers

Color

Cost

Groom

Flowers

Color

Cost

Best man/ushers

Quantity

Flowers

Color

Cost

Ring Bearer

Pillow: Details

Flowers

Color

Cost

Boutonniere: Details

Flowers

Color

Cost

Fathers

Quantity
Flowers
Color
Cost

Other boutonnieres

Quantity
Flowers
Color
Cost

Going away corsage

Quantity
Flowers
Color
Cost

TOTAL PERSONAL FLOWERS: $

REHEARSAL DINNER FLOWERS

Bride's corsage

Flowers
Color
Cost

Mothers' corsages

Quantity
Flowers
Color
Cost

Centerpieces

Quantity
Flowers

Color
Cost

TOTAL REHEARSAL DINNER: $

RECEPTION FLOWERS

Head Table
Details
Quantity
Flowers
Color
Cost

Guest Tables
Details
Quantity
Flowers
Color
Cost

Buffet tables
Details
Quantity
Flowers
Color
Cost

Wedding cake
Details
Quantity
Flowers
Color
Cost

Cake knife
Details
Quantity

Flowers
Color
Cost

Guest book table
Details
Quantity
Flowers
Color
Cost

Gift table
Details
Quantity
Flowers
Color
Cost

Floral/ivy garland
Details
Quantity
Flowers
Color
Cost

Restrooms
Details
Quantity
Flowers
Color
Cost

Other
Details
Quantity
Flowers

Color
Cost

TOTAL RECEPTION $

RENTED FROM FLORIST

Arch
Details
Quantity
Flowers
Color
Cost

Candelabra
Details
Quantity
Flowers
Color
Cost

Aisle runner
Details
Quantity
Flowers
Color
Cost

Wishing well or other envelope holder
Details
Quantity
Flowers
Color
Cost

Potted plants/topiaries
Details
Quantity

Flowers
Color
Cost

TOTAL RENTALS $

TOTAL:

Ceremony Flowers: $
Personal Flowers: $
Rehearsal dinner: $
Reception flowers: $
Rentals: $

Subtotal: $
Taxes: $
Delivery fee: $

GRAND TOTAL $

Deposit:

Date
Amount
Balance
Balance due date

For Your Notes

CHAPTER 7

Wedding Photography And Videography

The Photographer

Book your wedding photographer early in the planning stages. His (or her) work will form the tangible memories of your wedding day for years to come.

It is impossible to work with a photographer if your personalities clash. You will force your smiles without even realizing it, and it will show in the photographs. Find someone whose personality you like as well as their work.

Hire a photographer who has a back-up in case of illness or an unexpected emergency. Otherwise, you may have to hire a last-minute replacement. This will be sure to cost more, and you'll have no time to check references.

There are many new cameras on the market; professional photographers are the experts in how to use them and which camera to use for each shot. That is why you will often see them bring several cameras to a wedding. This has the added advantage of ensuring that a back-up camera is ready in case of equipment malfunction. Since I am not an expert on this new technology, I won't delve into the subject here. The photographer can show you the effects that can be obtained from each.

Many photographers specialize in "classic photography" (posed portraits) or "photojournalism" (pictures that show the events at the wedding). Find someone who is good at both.

Some churches do not allow photographs, yet most are sympathetic to the fact that you want to have photographs of your wedding ceremony. They will probably let the photographer take pictures (without flash) from the rear of the church. This is where zoom lenses come in. The biggest advantage is that you can get your close-ups but also a view of your guests as well.

Coverage differs, so clarify when the photographer will begin and finish. You will want him there until you leave the reception, or until your last dance.

The Videographer

Most couples want their wedding video to be a documentary of their wedding day. Cameras are becoming smaller and less intrusive than ever. I recommend two cameras, since it is impossible for a videographer to be in two places at once. With the two-camera method, you can have one videographer document the bride getting ready for the wedding while the other is filming the groom. As well, you can get two perspectives of the same moment.

If possible, hire a photographer and videographer from the same company. Still photos from the photographer can be added to the video. As well, the cost is often lower.

As with the photographer, the videographer's personality must match yours in order for you to work well together.

Ask to see a video that he has shot. This will show how he incorporates music, titles, and special effects. Some include childhood photos of the bride and groom.

Have voiceovers taped, so that they can be edited into the final video. For example, during the father-daughter dance, your father's voice can be heard reminiscing about your childhood.

Have the videographer interview the guests. This will become your favorite part of the video, and guests love the opportunity to send their messages and best wishes to you. Some videographers will edit a soundtrack into the final cut.

Special effects can sometimes get out of hand, so ask that these be used sparingly. Slow fades and dissolves are popular. A red rose can show up in an otherwise black and white sequence. The star filter turns each candle flame into a beautiful star!

Editing produces a smoothly-flowing and professional documentary of the day, but ask for an additional, unedited copy. The outtakes are so funny!

Coverage

Photography coverage for most weddings involves three locations: the church, outdoors, and the reception. Many wedding venues feature beautifully landscaped grounds for the purpose of wedding pictures. Most towns and cities also have parks with fountains, gazebos, and luxurious gardens.

If you are being married in a major city, the photographer might take you out onto the street for "Paris" shots. These dramatic photos, shot in black and white, are designed to show a strong European flavor.

Editing

Before you receive the pictures from the photographer, they will be edited. This involves many processes:

- Adjusting the light
- Airbrushing faces
- Removing red eye
- Cropping
- Removing unwanted objects from the picture

Packages

Photographers and videographers offer packages of their most popular services. If you hire both from the same company, they may be included in the same package, or you may get a separate package from each.

These packages consist of a set number of hours' coverage, albums for you and your parents, extra copies of the wedding video, photo enlargements, thank-you cards, and even framing services.

Packages offer substantial savings over the same services priced separately. However, they are not a saving if you don't need them. Sometimes, but not always, you will be allowed to substitute. Otherwise, chose only what you need.

Must-Have Photographs

- Bride putting on veil
- Bride with maid of honor
- Bride with flowers and bridesmaids
- Bride putting on garter
- Close-up of bride
- Full length of bride
- Bride with ring bearer and flower girl
- Bride with parents
- Invitation
- Bride and father leaving for church
- Bride in limousine
- Groom with best man
- Close-up of groom
- Full length of groom
- Groom with ushers
- Groom with parents
- Groom with rings
- Guests arriving
- Processional
- Ceremony sequence (close-up and overall views)
- Recessional
- Bridal party
- Bride and groom in limousine
- Close-up of bride and groom
- Hands and wedding rings
- Close-up of bouquets
- Receiving line

- Head table
- Bridal party with parents
- Speeches and toasts
- Cake cutting
- First dance
- Bride's dance with father
- Groom's dance with mother
- Wedding party dancing
- Parents' dance
- Bride throwing bouquet
- Groom throwing garter
- Last dance
- Bride and groom leaving reception
- List any special people you want to have photograph

Must-Have Video Shots

- Bride putting on veil
- Bride with maid of honor
- Bride with flowers and bridesmaids
- Bride putting on garter
- Close-up of bride
- Full length of bride
- Bride with ring bearer and flower girl
- Bride with parents
- Invitation
- Bride and father leaving for church
- Bride in limousine
- Groom with best man
- Close-up of groom
- Full length of groom
- Groom with ushers
- Groom with parents
- Groom with rings
- Guests arriving
- Processional
- Ceremony sequence (close-up and overall views)

- Recessional
- Bridal party
- Bride and groom in limousine
- Close-up of bride and groom
- Hands and wedding rings
- Close-up of bouquets
- Receiving line
- Head table
- Bridal party with parents
- Speeches and toasts
- Cake cutting
- First dance
- Bride's dance with father
- Groom's dance with mother
- Parents' dance
- Wedding party dancing
- Bride throwing bouquet
- Groom throwing garter
- Last dance
- Bride and groom leaving reception
- List any special people you want to have in video

For Your Notes

CHAPTER

8

Transportation For The Wedding Day

Limousines

The most popular type of wedding transportation is the chauffeur-driven limousine. The limousine company can help you decide between a standard or stretch limo, based on your needs.

When interviewing limousine companies, ask how they operate. Most companies begin and end their fee at the limousine's point of departure. Call several companies in your area to be sure you're getting the best deal.

Depending upon the setup of the company, it may be less expensive to rent the limo twice, to avoid paying for the time the driver and car are waiting during the reception. Some companies don't offer the option. Investigate and do your math.

Get the cell or pager number of your driver, and give him yours. It's good to be in constant touch with the limo in case of breakdowns or misplaced directions.

Vintage Cars

Vintage cars are second in popularity. They can be from a particular era, such as the 1940s or 1950s, or perhaps from your year of birth. Or, maybe you dream of a Rolls Royce.

Contact a local club or association for car buffs. Among their members, you will likely find someone willing to rent his car. Since many of these car owners are very protective of their "babies," you may just have a chauffeur included!

Horse and Buggy

Horse and buggy rides to and from the church are charming and romantic. For a Victorian or medieval theme wedding they are a necessity! Since they are subject to the weather, plan an alternative form of transportation as a backup. Be certain to ask about their refund policies in the event of inclement weather.

Private Transportation

Often, friends and family offer to do the wedding-day driving. This is a great favor for the bride and groom who don't want the expense of rented transportation. Pay for gas and car washes, unless the friend makes it clear that this is a wedding gift to you. Always find a backup who is willing to stand by (with a full tank of gas) in case of any unforeseen problems.

Calculating Transportation Needs

The bride and her father ride from home to the church. On the way to the reception, the bride and the groom ride together, the father with his wife.

The mother of the bride leaves about fifteen minutes before the bride. She can ride alone, with the bridesmaids, or with a friend or relative of her choice.

The groom and best man ride to the church together.

The groom rides from the church to the reception with the bride. The entire wedding party often rides in the limo with them. If not, the ushers usually drive the bridesmaids from the church to the reception.

However, many use their own cars, since they will be returning home quite late.

Out-of-town guests staying at a hotel may be able to get transportation by hotel van. For a large wedding, it may be practical to rent a shuttle bus to transport guests.

Transportation Routing Sheet

Company or individual
Driver
Cell phone

TRIP 1:

Transportation for:
Time: Pick up:
Drive to:
Return to:

TRIP 2:

Transportation for:
Time: Pick up:
Drive to:
Return to:

TRIP 3:

Transportation for:
Time: Pick up:
Drive to:
Return to:

For Your Notes

CHAPTER 9

Music for the Ceremony and Reception

Music for the Wedding Ceremony

You may be surprised to hear that *Here Comes the Bride* is forbidden at some wedding ceremonies! Make an appointment to meet with both the clergy and the organist or musical director before making any definite music plans. Although they are becoming more relaxed, there are still some churches that will not allow secular (non-religious) music.

The ceremony music can be performed by an organist, soloist, choir, brass or string ensemble, trumpet, piano, flute, or classical guitar. It is divided into five main categories. Let's look at each one separately.

The prelude music is played softly as the guests are seated. It begins twenty to thirty minutes before the ceremony. If a soloist or choir will be singing, plan this as the last piece of the prelude to change the mood somewhat and let guests know that the ceremony is nearing. As well, it acts as an audible signal to the wedding party that they are to take their places for the processional.

The processional music is played as the wedding party walks down the aisle. Depending on the length of the piece and the size of the wedding party, two pieces can be played. In this case, the entire wedding party will walk down the aisle and take their places at the altar during the first piece. The organist will play the second as the bride walks down the aisle. If only one piece of music will be used, the organist will be aware of the timing of the bride's entrance, so that the volume or the depth of the music can be increased for her.

The interlude music is played during the signing of the register, communion, and any other appropriate time. It is often different in nature, perhaps a solo or a flute piece.

The recessional music is played as the bride and groom lead the wedding party and guests out of the church. It is played with great fanfare.

The postlude follows the recessional and is played softly in the background until the last guests have left the church.

Popular wedding music consists generally of hymns and pieces of classical music.

- *Ave Maria*, by Bach
- *Ave Maria*, by Schubert
- *The Four Seasons*, by Vivaldi
- *Trumpet Voluntary*, by Clarke
- *Jesu, Joy of Man's Desiring*, by Bach
- *Water Music*, by Handel
- *Air on a G String*, by Bach
- *Ode to Joy*, by Beethoven
- *Canon in D*, by Pachelbel
- *Praise, My Soul, the King of Heaven*, by Goss
- *The Wedding March*, by Mendelssohn
- *Bridal Chorus (Here Comes the Bride)*, by Wagner

The clergy can recommend soloists who are familiar with the acoustics of their particular church. Audition with the actual piece you want the soloist to sing.

Occasionally, a groom will sing a special song to his bride. I have only once had a bride who wanted to sing at her wedding. We tried to talk her out of it, worried that she would be too nervous to follow through. She insisted, though, and did a beautiful rendition of *Only God Could Love You More*.

Disc Jockeys

Fees for disc jockey services vary widely and so do the services that they will provide. Investigate independent DJs and the DJ companies. Although it costs more to use a company that hires out more than one DJ, a sudden emergency simply means they will send out a different person. If an independent DJ cancels at the last minute, you will have to scramble to find a new one; not all have backups available.

Before your wedding date, meet with the DJ to go over your choices of music for the special dances. Note any songs that you do *not* want played, such as songs that bring back unpleasant memories.

Your DJ will usually be willing to act as Master of Ceremonies if you do not have someone else in mind.

Musicians

When we speak of "musicians," we can mean so many things: a string quartet, a wind trio, a single piano player, or a full band for the reception. Obviously this is the more expensive option, as their fee is used to pay each band member.

Audition musicians in person. If this is not possible, they will provide you with a demo CD. Be sure that the musicians you hear are actually the ones who will be playing at the wedding. Membership in a union will affect their contract with you. Have all details in writing, including the number and length of breaks, setup times, mileage charges, and attire.

Music for the Reception

The music for your wedding reception consists of background music during dinner, music for dancing, and music to be played at specific times, such as when you throw your bouquet.

During dinner, keep the mood relaxed. Classical music would not be out of place here, but light popular music is more appropriate. Include Broadway show tunes and favorites from such performers as Elton John and Billy Joel. Played on a grand piano, without lyrics, they are relaxing and yet upbeat enough to suit every taste.

Dancing is a part of most wedding celebrations, with the exception of small cocktail receptions. The most special dance, of course, is the first dance that you and your new husband will share as a married couple.

Most couples spend a great deal of time choosing the song for this dance. You may wish to use "your song." A word of warning–there are many popular songs that seem like love songs, but they are not. A common example is *Every Breath You Take* by The Police. The lyrics are about obsession and surveillance. Many couples choose Whitney Houston's *I Will Always Love You*, without realizing that it is about the end of a relationship.

Regardless of your taste in music, the first dance is usually slow. You may wish to choose from a list of popular first dance songs. Your DJ can show you one. These lists include:

- *From This Moment,* by Shania Twain
- *Can I Have This Dance?* by Anne Murray
- *Everything I Do,* by Bryan Adams
- *Unforgettable,* by Natalie Cole
- *We've Only Just Begun*, by The Carpenters
- *The Way You Look Tonight*, by Frank Sinatra
- *Just the Way You Are*, by Billy Joel
- *Groovy Kind of Love*, by Phil Collins
- *The Power of Love*, by Celine Dion

Guests frequently circle the bride and groom and applaud at the conclusion of this dance. You can dance to this song in its entirety and be joined by others for the second song, or you can have others cut in during this dance. It's entirely your choice. If you prefer, the second dance can be just for you and your father, thereby moving your groom and his mother into the third song.

Whatever the length of the dances, the order of the other couples is consistent. Adjust the following list to suit your needs, and be sure that each member of the wedding party is aware of this order:

- Bride and Groom
- Bride with Dad
- Groom with Mom

- Parents
- Wedding party
- All guests

In the event that a parent is unable to dance for physical reasons, or if the parent is deceased, that part of the dance can be eliminated, or perhaps another family member would be honored to fill in. Discuss any special situations with all involved. You may wish to have your stepfather cut in halfway through your dance with your father if your relationship with him has been especially close.

The DJ will have all of the popular favorites in his collection. If you want a special song that is not well known, supply the DJ with the recording and he will play it at the appropriate time. DJs are happy to take requests from you and your guests. As well, they will gladly work from a list of your favorite songs.

A variety of musical styles will ensure that there is literally "something for everyone." These styles include 1950s and 1960s rock and roll, disco/dance music, music from the Big Bands of the 1940s, and easy listening music. Often, a waltz or polka is played for those who enjoy such dances. Inform the DJ ahead of time about the age mix of the group. Cater to the musical tastes of your older guests. Just because you and your friends are young, doesn't mean that you can play ear-splitting music all evening!

Your last dance will be similar in mood to your first. It has become a custom for the guests to form a circle around the bride and groom during this dance. Afterwards, you go around the circle, greeting each person and thanking them for attending. In a variation of this tradition, the guests hold hands and swarm in on the couple several times during this dance. My feelings are that this spoils a beautiful and romantic moment, but no one means any harm. If you do not want this at your wedding, have several friends spread the word.

Popular Songs for the Father/Daughter Dance

For the dance between the bride and her father, and the groom and his mother, slow and sentimental songs are usually chosen. I say "usually" because I once had a father and daughter choose Glenn Miller's *In the Mood.* Common choices include:

- *Hero*, by Mariah Carey
- *You Are The Sunshine of My Life*, by Stevie Wonder
- *What a Wonderful World*, by Louis Armstrong
- *Can You Feel the Love Tonight*, by Elton John
- *I'll Be There*, by Mariah Carey
- *In My Life*, by The Beatles
- *Because You Loved Me*, by Celine Dion
- *The Long and Winding Road*, by The Beatles
- *Lean On Me*, by Bill Withers
- *Bridge Over Troubled Water*, by Art Garfunkel
- *Butterfly Kisses*, by Bob Carlisle
- *The Greatest Love of All*, by Whitney Houston
- *Wind Beneath My Wings*, by Bette Midler
- *Isn't She Lovely*, by Stevie Wonder

Popular Songs for the Mother/Son Dance

- *A Song for Mama*, by Boyz II Men
- *A Song for My Son*, by Mikki Viereck / Ray Allure
- *Close to You*, by The Carpenters
- *Evergreen*, by Barbra Streisand
- *Have I Told You Lately*, by Van Morrison
- *I Hope You Dance*, by Lee Ann Womack
- *Moonlight Serenade*, by Glenn Miller
- *Rock and Roll Lullaby*, by B. J. Thomas
- *Sunrise Sunset*, by Topol
- *The Impossible Dream*, by Luther Vandross
- *The Long and Winding Road*, by The Beatles
- *The Rose*, by Bette Midler
- *Through the Years*, by Kenny Rogers
- *Till the End of Time*, by Perry Como
- *Times of Your Life*, by Paul Anka
- *What a Wonderful World*, by Louis Armstrong
- *You Decorated My Life*, by Kenny Rogers
- *You're the Inspiration*, by Chicago

Ceremony Music Worksheet

Prelude (approximately 20 minutes) Indicate if the piece is to be sung by a soloist

1.
2.
3.
4.

Last prelude piece (to be an audible signal that the processional is about to begin)

Processional

Bridesmaids and Maid of Honor

Bride

Signing of the Register

Recessional

Postlude

Reception Music Worksheet

Pre-dinner music:

1.
2.
3.
4.

Background music during dinner:

1.
2.
3.
4.
5.
6.

Special dances:

Bride and Groom

Bride and Father

Groom and Mother

Wedding party

Parents

Bride and Groom's last dance

Other music:

Garter

Bouquet

Special requests:

1.
2.
3.
4.
5.

For Your Notes

CHAPTER 10

Rehearsal and Rehearsal Dinner

The Rehearsal

It was once considered unlucky for a bride to rehearse her own wedding. She would sit in a pew while a friend acted as a stand-in. Margaret Truman changed that by insisting on participating in her own wedding rehearsal.

Try to schedule the rehearsal a couple of days before the wedding, especially if the celebration afterward will keep you up too late. This is not always possible, though, and the rehearsal and rehearsal dinner are usually held the night before the wedding.

When you booked the ceremony date, you also booked the date for the rehearsal. Arrive fifteen minutes early, so that you do not keep the clergy waiting. After a prayer, he will turn the rehearsal over to your wedding planner (if you have one) or he may prefer to handle it himself.

There are many ways to coordinate the rehearsal. This way works well for most weddings, but allow the clergy or wedding planner to guide you.

Begin at the altar, and have the bridesmaids and groomsmen line up as they will be standing during the ceremony. In a Christian wedding, the bridesmaids are on the left and the groomsmen on the right, although some may prefer to have them in alternating positions. They are usually lined up according to height, with the tallest closest to the maid of honor and best man, but this can also be reversed. If you have husband and wife attendants, you may decide to ignore the height so that they will be paired up during the recessional. This is the time to determine whether the groomsmen will have their hands at the front, back, or side. They must all do the same.

For a Jewish ceremony, the groom and best man stand under the chuppah, on the left side, with his parents behind him and the ushers off to the side. The bride and maid of honor stand under the chuppah, on the right side, with her parents behind her and the bridesmaids off to the side.

At this point, assign letters to the bridesmaids and groomsmen. The two beside the best man and maid of honor are "A," the two beside them are "B," etc.

If the organist is present at the rehearsal, play the recessional music, and the wedding party will practice walking toward the back of the church in this order:

- Bride and Groom
- Maid of Honor and Best Man
- Flower Girl and Ring Bearer
- Bridesmaid A and Groomsman A
- Bridesmaid B and Groomsman B, etc.

Decide whether the flower girl and ring bearer will stand at the altar or rejoin their parents. If they sit with their parents during the service, they will not be part of the recessional.

At this point you will be at the back of the church. Points to cover (in order) are:

- Seating the groom's grandparents
- Seating the bride's grandparents
- Seating the groom's parents
- Seating the bride's mother
- Two ushers pull the aisle runner
- Signal organist to play music chosen for the processional
- Clergy, groom, best man, and groomsmen take their places at the altar
- Bridesmaids C, then B, then A walk down the aisle and take their places
- Maid of honor walks down the aisle and takes her place
- Flower girl and ring bearer
- Bride and father

You will walk on your father's right arm, so that he will not have to walk around you to get to his seat. This is especially important if you are wearing a long train.

At this point, the clergy will guide the wedding party through the components of the ceremony, although he will not be reading the actual service.

The processional and recessional will now be rehearsed again, meaning that you have gone through both twice. It is important that all parts of the wedding be rehearsed. Bring along candles to practice lighting the unity candle; use a light bulb to practice the breaking of the glass. Have the wedding party rehearse kneeling at the rail and walking around the altar. Use a mock bouquet to practice handing it to your maid of honor. Bring the aisle runner to the rehearsal so the ushers can practice pulling it.

If your gown has a train, you will move quite differently. It will be necessary to take wide turns. Thread ribbon through the top of a lace curtain and tie it around your waist so that you can practice turning and your maid of honor can practice straightening it.

After the rehearsal is over, you will all celebrate at the rehearsal dinner. It is customary to invite the clergy and the wedding planner to this dinner. Whether or not they attend is up to them.

The Rehearsal Dinner

The groom's parents host the rehearsal dinner. They issue the invitations verbally, approximately two weeks before the dinner. The immediate families, all members of the wedding party, their significant others, and the parents of the ring bearer and flower girl are invited. If any friends or family have had to travel a great distance to attend the wedding, include them as well.

The groom's father proposes the first toast. He welcomes the guests and thanks whoever will be hosting the wedding. The father of the bride makes the next toast, then the best man, and finally any members of the wedding party who wish to do so. The bride and groom may also propose a toast if they wish.

Be sure to wrap up the rehearsal dinner at a reasonable hour. I suggest ordering just one pre-dinner drink; God forbid any member of the wedding party should be hung-over the next day!

Rehearsal Worksheet

Date

Time

Location

Bring the following objects with you:

- This book
- Marriage license (if you haven't already given it to your officiant)
- Practice bouquet
- Practice train
- Unity candles
- Light bulb (for Jewish weddings)
- Aisle runner
- All checklists
- The shoes you will be wearing
- Rings
- Vows, if you are writing your own
- CD player and a CD of wedding music, if necessary

Notes

Rehearsal Dinner Worksheet

Date
Time

LOCATION

Address
Telephone
Contact person
Reservation confirmed

Number attending

Music

Flowers

Caterer

Toasts

MENU

Appetizers
Soup/salad
Main course
Dessert
Beverages (alcoholic and nonalcoholic)

Notes

Rehearsal Dinner Guest list

Make as many copies of this page as you need

Name
Address
Telephone
Attending?

Name
Address
Telephone
Attending?

Name
Address
Telephone
Attending?

Name
Address
Telephone
Attending?

Name
Address
Telephone
Attending?

For Your Notes

CHAPTER 11

The Countdown Begins!

The Night Before

With the rehearsal dinner, visiting with relatives, and the general excitement of these past weeks and months, you may find that you're too wound up to fall asleep easily! Do not be lured into the trap of a sleeping pill or a nightcap; you will regret it tomorrow morning. Instead, try warm milk and a boring book. A hot bath before you go to bed may also help.

The secret here is to rest if you can't sleep. That's what I do on overnight flights to Europe when I have to hit the ground running. You will manage to fall asleep, and awake to realize that your wedding day has finally arrived!

Brides have been known to faint due to nerves and empty stomachs. You may not get another chance to eat until the reception dinner, so *please* try to have some breakfast.

Part of the fun of the wedding day is meeting up with your bridesmaids to get dressed together. You can do this at your parents' home or at the church. You will also go with your girls to have your hair done. If you will be to going to the church to arrange the flowers for the ceremony, take the programs and wedding bubbles with you.

At some point during the morning, remember to switch your engagement ring to your right hand, where it will remain until after the ceremony.

Hair, Makeup, and Nails

Although the bride's hairstyle is always left in the hands of her hairstylist, you will have your say. It is important to consider your hairstyle when choosing your headpiece and veil.

Go with a style that is close to your usual. If you make drastic changes to your appearance you will look unfamiliar in your wedding photos. Many brides look absolutely regal with their hair up.

Choose your headpiece according to how it looks as an accessory to your gown, and how well it accentuates the shape of your face. From there, you can work with your stylist to come up with the perfect hairstyle.

- **Oval face:** The best styles for you, in both hairstyle and headpiece/ veil, are those that frame the face. A minimum of hair height and a maximum of width midway between the eye and the jaw, such a layered style, would be most flattering.
- **Round face:** Add height to minimize fullness. This can be done by having the hair fall below the jaw line.
- **Square face:** A long veil and long hairstyle both work well with this face shape. Minimize the width, but create height at the top.
- **Heart-shaped face:** Both the hairstyle and the veil should minimize the width at the side and create height at the top as well as volume at the chin. Bangs look great with this face shape.

If you will be doing your own hair, practice in advance. Time yourself so you'll know how long it will take on the morning of the wedding. Some brides prefer to have the hair stylist come to their home. Be sure you have a proper place to work; you need good lighting and an electrical outlet.

During the peak wedding season, stylists book up quickly, so make your appointment about two months in advance. Prior to that, set up an appointment for a practice session. That way you can see what the style will look like and the stylist will be able to advise you if it needs changing.

If you book an appointment for your wedding party, be sure to specify how many will be there. You cannot show up with even one extra person.

Do not depart too much from your usual makeup. However, you will definitely wear more than usual on your wedding day. A professional makeup artist is accustomed to working with photographers, and can advise you on the best look for your wedding photos.

Nail polish that is natural or pink looks best in photographs. In black and white photos, red lipstick appears black. Neutral shades look best. Frosted eye shadows and lipsticks shine in the camera's flash.

A bride who wears glasses should choose her headpiece and hairstyle accordingly. Many brides try to go without their glasses on their wedding day, but remember that people are used to seeing you with them. On the other hand, if you have been thinking about getting contact lenses, allow plenty of time to adjust to them.

Dressing for the Wedding

After all these months of waiting, it's finally time for you to put on your wedding gown! You will need someone to help you get dressed. This is usually the maid of honor, but it can also be your mother, one of the bridesmaids, or your sister. Put a white sheet on the floor to protect the gown.

Always step into the gown. If the style is such that you must put it on over your head, place a pillowcase over your head to avoid makeup coming into contact with the gown.

Have your helper zip, lace, or button your gown. A crochet hook helps if you have button loops. Lacing must not be too loose or too tight.

First Aid for the Wedding Gown

Every bride's worse nightmare is to have her dress caught in a greasy car door. If you should be so unfortunate, place a paper towel on a hard surface and blot the stain facedown, feathering at the edges. Hopefully this will take out the stain; if not, repeat the process. Follow with soap and water and blot dry.

Blood can be removed by dropping hydrogen peroxide onto the spot with an eyedropper, blotting, and repeating as necessary.

Sprinkling a spill of red wine with salt will neutralize it, and it can then be blotted with a white towel.

If you should get ink on your gown, rub the spot with hairspray on a cotton ball.

Oil stains, such as those from perfume or even your dinner, can be removed by applying white chalk, talcum powder, or cornstarch. After fifteen or twenty minutes, the oil will be absorbed and can be blotted with a clean white towel.

If the gown is creased before the wedding, steam it by hanging it in the bathroom for several minutes with the hot water turned on full. Avoid direct contact with the water. For smaller wrinkles, use a steamer. If water should splash on the gown, iron the spot.

Every fabric is different, and there is no guarantee that these techniques will work on your gown. They will not remove the spot completely, but will make it less noticeable. Before leaving the bridal boutique, ask the staff for recommendations.

Bride's Last Minute Checklist

- Wedding gown
- Veil, headpiece
- Underwear, extra stockings
- Shoes
- Jewelry
- Hair appointment made
- Manicure appointment made
- Make up appointment made
- Going-away outfit, including underwear, shoes, jewelry
- Honeymoon suitcase(s) packed
- Wedding night bag packed
- Garter
- Penny for shoe
- Extra shoes (for dancing)
- Ring pillow
- Copy of vows
- Groom's ring
- Unity candle
- Programs
- Place cards
- Emergency kit

Groom's Last Minute Checklist

- Rented formal wear
- Shoes
- Cufflinks
- Hair cut appointment made
- Going-away clothes
- Nail clippers/file
- Honeymoon suitcase(s) packed
- Wedding night bag packed
- Money and credit cards
- Honeymoon itinerary
- Bride's ring
- Cuticle scissors (to remove ring from pillow)
- Envelope for officiant (give it to the best man)
- Cash gifts for those helping at wedding
- Checks for vendors requiring payment
- Marriage license (many churches require you to give it to them several days in advance of the wedding)
- Copy of vows

Your Emergency Kit

Your wedding planner will have a bag of items that will save the day in case of an emergency. In case you don't have a wedding planner, put together one of your own. Start with the following items, and add whatever else you see fit:

- stain remover
- degreaser
- Aspirin or Tylenol
- pantyhose, beige
- mini pads, tampons
- several dollars in change
- tissues
- bobby pins
- toothbrush and toothpaste
- gum or mints
- glue
- corsage pins
- Band-Aids
- zipper-closure plastic bags
- cell phone
- hand lotion
- baby powder
- wet wipes
- hair spray
- perfume
- nail file
- cotton balls
- brush and comb
- make-up kit
- small sewing kit
- umbrella
- mirror
- travel iron
- hand-held steamer
- hair dryer
- curling iron

Wedding Day Timeline

This timeline will be helpful when filling out the wedding day schedule, which follows. Items can be changed or deleted as necessary.

1 to 2 hours prior to the ceremony:
- Bridesmaids arrive to dress
- Note location (bride's home, church, etc.)

1 hour prior to the ceremony:
- Photographer arrives
- Note location, as above
- Ushers arrive at church

1 hour prior to the ceremony:
- Bridesmaids and mother of the bride leave for the church
- Bride and her father leave for the church
- Candles are lighted and prelude music begins
- Groom, best man, and clergy arrive at church (note which room)

15 minutes prior to the ceremony:
- Parents, bridesmaids and bride arrive at church (note which room)

10 minutes prior to the ceremony:
- Soloist
- Grandparents of the groom are seated

8 minutes prior to the ceremony:
- Grandparents of the bride are seated

5 minutes prior to the ceremony:
- Parents of the groom are seated

3 minutes prior to the ceremony:
- Mother of the bride is seated

1 minute prior to ceremony:
- Ushers pull the aisle runner
- Enter groom, best man, and clergy

Exact hour of ceremony:
- Processional
- Ceremony
- Recessional

Immediately after ceremony:

Photographs

Approximately 1 hour after the ceremony:

Bride and groom arrive at reception

Receiving line

1 hour later:

Dinner is served

Toasts

Immediately after dinner:

First dance

2 hours before the end of booking:

Cake cutting

1 hour before the end of booking:

Bouquet and garter

45 minutes before the end of booking:

Bride and groom depart

Wedding Day Schedule

Feel free to delete any items that do not apply to your wedding. After all, you have enough to think about today!

_:_ Wake, shower, breakfast
_:_ Hair and makeup
_:_ Bridesmaids arrive to dress at:
_:_ Photographer arrives at:
_:_ Ushers arrive at church
_:_ Bridesmaids, mother of the bride leave for church
_:_ Bride and father leave for church
_:_ Groom, best man, and clergy meet at church
_:_ Candles are lighted, organist and soloist take their places, prelude music begins
_:_ Grandparents of the groom are seated
_:_ Grandparents of the bride are seated
_:_ Parents of the groom are seated
_:_ Mother of the bride is seated
_:_ Signal to ushers to pull the aisle runner
_:_ Enter groom, best man, and clergy
_:_ Processional, ceremony, recessional
_:_ Photographs
_:_ Bride and groom arrive at reception
_:_ Receiving line
_:_ Dinner is served
_:_ First dance
_:_ Cake cutting
_:_ Bouquet and garter
_:_ Bride and groom depart
_:_ Booking ends

For Your Notes

CHAPTER

12

The Ceremony

The wedding ceremony is the most sacred part of the day. It is not a theatrical performance; it is the moment when you and your groom are joined together as man and wife. Of course you want it to be perfect, and it will be in your eyes. Just be careful not to lose sight of its true meaning as you make your way through this chapter.

Location

The majority of weddings are held in a house of worship, usually that of the bride and/or groom. Some churches will only marry members; others are more relaxed. If the church is not one to which you belong, investigate the restrictions and regulations before asking to meet with the clergy.

Home weddings are (and always have been) popular. They can be held indoors, often using a fireplace as an altar. They can also be held in the garden. In this case, a tent will be your insurance against bad weather.

Hotel ceremonies can be held in the same room as the reception. The bride and groom will mingle with guests elsewhere while the room is "turned." This means that the chairs from the wedding ceremony will be removed and placed around tables for the dinner.

Many historic locations, mansions, castles, and even museums can be rented for wedding ceremonies. Most offer beautiful gardens, but an indoor wedding at one of these locations is equally stunning.

In order to marry at a private club, the bride or groom (or their parents) must often be members. However, many will open their facilities to the paying public. Some even have facilities designed for the purpose, such as wedding gazebos.

If you have booked a reception hall, the wedding and reception can be held at the same location. Some reception facilities feature charming chapels which are used for ceremonies. Others can accommodate garden weddings.

Beaches and parks are romantic and popular settings for outdoor weddings.

Working with the Clergy

The particular denomination of the church will determine whether you will have to go to mandatory counseling or classes. The clergy will also have a set of rules and policies pertaining to wedding ceremonies. These include such items as throwing birdseed and confetti, playing secular music, picture taking during the ceremony, and using thumbtacks or nails on the woodwork.

Be prepared to meet several times with the clergy over the course of the wedding planning process. If you will be writing your own vows, have the priest look them over.

If you wish to have a Catholic ceremony in a location other than in the church, your priest might be able to refer you to someone in the Old Catholic Church, which originated in the 1700s and expanded to North America in the early 1900s. The orders and sacraments are recognized by the Roman Catholic Church and the faith is almost identical to the mainstream Catholic Church although they are not in communion with Catholic Church, don't recognize the Pope, and report to their own Bishops.

The Marriage License

It is important that you familiarize yourself with the laws of your area. Find out what medical and blood tests are necessary, which documents must be presented, and what waiting period (if any) there is.

Identification in the form of a birth certificate or passport must be shown. If either or both of you are divorced, proof must be presented. If the divorce took place in a different country, you may have to get a lawyer's letter as proof that the divorce is legal in the area in which you wish to be married.

The marriage license can be purchased at your local City Hall or municipal offices. Call ahead for hours and fees. Pick up the application in advance and fill it in at your leisure.

Most couples go together to get the marriage license and then have a celebratory lunch afterward. Sometimes, however, it is necessary for one of you to go alone. Check ahead to be sure your local office allows this. In this case, the absent person must fill out his or her section of the application accurately, including a signature, and send along a passport or birth certificate and proof of a previous divorce.

The Religious Wedding Ceremony

Christian and Jewish wedding ceremonies, as well as those of other faiths and cultures, will be covered in detail in Chapter 14, Cultural and Religious Weddings. The religious ceremony often includes Scripture readings. Some of the more popular are these:

- Matthew 22:35-40
- Genesis 2:18-24
- 1 Corinthians 13:4-7
- Ephesians 5:25-32
- Romans 8:31-39
- Romans 12:1-2
- Matthew 5:1-12, 13-16
- Proverbs 31:10-13
- Hosea 2:21-22
- Ruth 1:6
- Song of Solomon 4:1-3
- Song of Solomon 5:10-14
- Isaiah 61:10
- Isaiah 62:5
- Hebrews 13:4
- Ecclesiastes 4:9-12

The Civil Ceremony

The civil ceremony is held at City Hall or in any other location of the couple's choosing. Some couples want to personalize this ceremony. This is usually permissible, but be sure to check first before you write your own vows, as the final decision will rest with the person performing the ceremony.

Civil ceremonies can be very simple or quite elaborate. Two witnesses are required for legal reasons, but many couples opt for a larger wedding party. Some couples invite guests. Brides often wear wedding gowns, although the usual dress for a civil ceremony is simpler.

The Non-Denominational Ceremony

The non-denominational ceremony differs from the civil ceremony in that it is a religious ceremony performed by clergy. However, it is performed in a manner that does not identify it as belonging to any religious denomination.

Couples choose non-denominational ceremonies if they are different denominations, or if they desire a religious ceremony despite the fact that they have no religious affiliations.

Childcare During the Ceremony

Children at a wedding are a major cause of disagreements. It is easy to see the point of view of guests who must travel some distance to attend the wedding and who do not want to leave their small children at home. It is also easy to understand the guests who cannot hear the ceremony because of a child who is bored or crying.

In order to provide a solution acceptable to everyone, I began years ago to offer childcare at weddings and receptions. This solution may work for your wedding, as well.

Hire someone who is able to handle children of all ages, from infants to school age. They must know first aid and CPR. Hire enough caregivers, especially if there will be children with special needs. Meet with the caregivers ahead of time and decide on a fee. You may wish to pay for the childcare as a courtesy to your guests, or the parents of the children can use the service on a pay-as-you-go basis. Many churches already have facilities for this very purpose. For the reception, the children should be close enough to the action that they do not feel too separated from their parents, yet far enough away that they can nap quietly.

Leave it up to the caregiver to choose activities for the children, but do not allow glue, paint, crayons, or scissors. Instead, have the caregivers provide toys and storybooks, as well as plenty of Disney videos. Many children will bring a toy from home. They should also bring a pillow and blanket, as it will be a late night for them.

Include the caregivers in your vendor meal head-count. They will eat with the children, of course.

Programs

Adding a program to the wedding ceremony is a lovely touch, as well as a way to convey valuable information. For example, it introduces members of the wedding party who may be unfamiliar to the guests. If the ceremony includes traditions of another faith or culture, the program can be used to explain these so that the guests can appreciate their meaning and symbolism.

Although programs can be professionally printed, this is one area in which it is possible to cut costs. Print the programs on your home computer, using some of the beautiful papers made just for this purpose.

If the program will be short, it can be printed on one page and folded or rolled into a scroll. Longer ones can be printed on several sheets and made into a booklet form. Details to include:

- The names of the wedding party and their relationship to you, such as "brother of the groom" or "college roommate of the bride"
- The names of those participating in the ceremony, such as the organist, readers, or soloist. Include the clergy here, too
- A tribute to a deceased friend or loved one
- A favorite prayer or Scripture passage which will be read during the ceremony

- A special message from you and your groom to your guests, thanking them for sharing the happiest day of your lives
- Any necessary reception information, such as directions to the reception, or perhaps a map

Plan on one program for each couple, plus extras for keepsakes. Some brides prefer one for each person. The ushers can hand them out as they seat the guests. Programs can also be mailed to anyone who was unable to attend the wedding.

Decorating for the Ceremony

The most important thing to remember is that the church or synagogue is a sacred place and that the decoration should act as a backdrop for the exchange of the marriage vows.

The more ornate the church or synagogue is, the less ornamentation should be applied. If the windows are not stained glass, place an arrangement on each windowsill. For a small ceremony, potted plants can be used to section the church. Short arrangements can be heightened by placing them on columns or pedestals.

Place pew bows on every pew or every second pew. Candelabra can be placed on each side of the altar. Drape the altar rail with ropes of flowers and ivy.

Under no circumstances are balloons considered to be tasteful ceremony decorations; use them for the reception if you like.

Aisle runners rarely stay in place if used on a tile or wooden floor, and they are unnecessary on carpeting. Nevertheless, they do add to the ambiance, so use one if you wish.

Writing Your Own Wedding Vows

If you and your groom want to write your own wedding vows, begin early to put your thoughts on paper and organize what you will say. Reflect on your feelings about love and marriage, how you met, and what has brought you to this point.

What you say is a highly personal matter; no matter what the vows say, you will still be legally married. Intersperse your own thoughts into the wording of a traditional wedding ceremony. Include references to your individual cultures and backgrounds, but avoid petty things and issues such as equality for women. These have no place in a wedding ceremony. Keep the vows to three minutes at the most.

Practice reading the vows aloud. What looks good on paper may turn out to be a tongue twister. Have the clergy hold a copy of the vows during the ceremony. That way, if either of you forgets, they can prompt you.

Illness or a Death in the Family

Most weddings take place without a thought to these realities of life, yet it is possible that any wedding could be affected, even yours. Each situation is unique and should be handled accordingly.

If you or your groom should fall ill, the wedding can often proceed as planned. Depending upon the illness, your family doctor may be able to give you some advice on covering up symptoms. Makeup can cover up quite a lot, too. If the illness is more serious, the wedding will have to be postponed. If there is no time to issue a printed notice, notify guests by telephone. If a new date has been set, include it in the notice.

If a close family member is ill, the nature of the illness will determine if the wedding should go on as planned or if it should be postponed. The wishes of the patient should also be considered. If the illness is terminal, it may be possible to move up the wedding date so that they may be included.

The death of a family member before the wedding presents the same dilemma. The family will have to weigh all their options and base their decision on such things as the age of the person, the length of the illness, and the cause of death. Again, the wishes of the deceased, if known, should be taken into consideration.

If the wedding will take place soon after a death, there are many ways to honor a deceased loved one. Place a rose in the pew where they would have been seated, print a memorial in the program, or place your wedding bouquet at the cemetery. A Roman Catholic bride can honor a deceased mother by placing her bouquet at the statue of the Blessed Virgin Mary.

Seating the Guests

Traditionally, friends and family of the bride sit on the left side of the aisle, and the friends and family of the groom on the right side for a Christian wedding. This is reversed for the Jewish wedding. The ushers can seat mutual friends of the bride and groom on either side to even up the numbers.

At a Christian wedding, the parents of the bride and groom sit in the front row of their particular side. For a Jewish wedding, the parents stand with their children under the chuppah.

If the church has two aisles, the bride's family and friends will sit on both sides of the left aisle, and the groom's family on both sides of the right aisle. The bride's parents will sit on the left side of the center section, and the groom's parents on the right side of the center section. Or, you may wish to use only one aisle.

The ushers will seat guests from the front to the back as they enter the church. After the bride's mother has been seated, there will be no more guests seated by the ushers. Those who arrive late can quietly let themselves into the back rows.

The first several rows are the "reserved" rows. The first is for the parents. The second is for grandparents and siblings. Special guests, such as godparents or the parents of the flower girl and ring bearer, occupy the third row. These guests will receive cards with their invitations that are known as "pew cards" as you remember from Chapter 5.

When the guests have all been seated, the groom's mother is escorted to her seat by an usher, followed by the groom's father. The bride's mother is then escorted to her seat, a signal that the ceremony is about to begin. Be sure that the ushers are aware of the correct way to escort guests to their seats.

- A couple: The usher offers his right arm to the lady, with her escort walking a few steps behind. If the couple has children, they walk with their father. However, if there are enough ushers, a teenaged girl would be thrilled to be escorted to her seat!

- Two ladies together: Each is escorted by an usher, unless there is a shortage of ushers. In this case, the usher will offer his right arm to the eldest, the other following a few steps behind.
- Men arriving alone: The usher does not offer his arm, but walks down the aisle beside the man to show him to his seat.

If divorced parents have not remarried and are still on friendly terms, they may sit together in the front pew. If one or both has remarried, the mother and her second husband sit in the first row; the father and his second wife sit in the third row (the second is for siblings). In a Jewish wedding, both parents are under the chuppah. Their spouses sit in the third row.

The Processional

The processional is the first glimpse the guests will have of you as you walk up the aisle toward your groom. The order in which the wedding party enters the church is more or less standard, with a couple of variations.

In the most popular Christian procession, the bridesmaids are followed by the maid of honor, then the flower girl and ring bearer together, and finally the bride with her father. The groom, best man, and ushers are waiting at the altar. If there are more than four bridesmaids, they can walk in pairs, with an odd-numbered bridesmaid centered behind the others. As a variation of this processional, the ushers walk in the processional singly or in pairs, ahead of the bridesmaids. Again, the groom and best man will be waiting at the altar.

Traditionally, the bride is escorted down the aisle by her father. However, this may not be a choice for you. Perhaps your father is deceased, or maybe you were never close while you were growing up. If you would like a substitute to walk you down the aisle, a stepfather, older brother, or favorite uncle can certainly fill the role. You may even be given away by your mother. You may also walk down the aisle alone or be met halfway by your groom, who will then walk the rest of the way with you. This is symbolic of the way your lives have been to this point and will continue afterward.

If you will be escorted up the aisle, you will be on your father's right arm. That way, he will not have to walk around you and risk stepping on your train as he takes his place in the front pew beside your mother. Many fathers give their daughters a kiss when they reach they altar. If you are wearing a face veil, he can lift it up slightly. That way, your groom can have the honor of folding it back when you are pronounced husband and wife.

The Jewish processional is quite different than that of Christian ceremonies. Here, the ushers lead the way down the aisle, followed by the best man, the groom with his parents, the bridesmaids, the maid of honor, and the bride with her parents. As the wedding party reaches the chuppah, they will fan out into the positions they took during the rehearsal. The bride will hand her bouquet to the maid of honor, who will hold it until the recessional.

While waiting for the processional to begin, everyone must stay out of sight of the guests, lined up in the order you rehearsed. As the wedding party walks up the aisle, they will be evenly spaced, between four and six paces apart.

If the church has two aisles, use one for the processional and the other for the recessional, so that everyone can get a good view of the wedding party. Examples of processionals follow on the next pages.

Examples of Processionals

Example 1

Example of a processional that includes the ushers

NOTE: The ushers and the bridesmaids are paired due to the size of the wedding party

Officiant/Groom/Best Man at altar
Usher/Usher
Usher/Usher
Usher/Usher
Bridesmaid/Bridesmaid
Bridesmaid/Bridesmaid
Bridesmaid/Bridesmaid
Maid of Honor
Flower Girl/Ring Bearer
Father of Bride/Bride

Example 2

Example of a processional that does not include the ushers

Officiant/Groom/Best Man/Ushers at altar
Bridesmaid
Bridesmaid
Bridesmaid
Maid of Honor
Flower Girl/Ring Bearer
Father of Bride/Bride

Example 3

Example of a Jewish processional

Usher/Usher
Usher/Usher
Best Man
Father/Groom/Mother
Bridesmaid/Bridesmaid
Bridesmaid/Bridesmaid
Maid of Honor
Father/Bride/Mother

Parts of the Ceremony (Christian)

- After the processional the wedding party is assembled at the altar.
- Call to Worship: "Dearly beloved, we are gathered here today …"
- Prayer, followed by a Scripture reading.
- Homily: This is optional; the clergy will share some additional thoughts on the subject of marriage.
- Declaration of Consent: "Who gives this woman to be married to this man?" If the bride is older or if this is her second marriage, her father does not give her away, although he may still walk her down the aisle.
- Additional Prayers or Readings, if desired.
- Groom's Vows: His own, or the traditional "Do you take this woman …" Bride's Vows: Her own, or the traditional "Do you take this man …"
- Blessing and Exchanging of Rings
- Pronouncement: "I now pronounce you man and wife. You may kiss the bride"
- Prayer: Usually the Lord's Prayer
- Soloist: As the bride and groom sign the register
- Unity candle: Both mothers light the side candles before the processional. The bride and groom now light the center candle, as a symbol of their new life together. Sometimes this is replaced by a sand ceremony. The bride and groom each pour different-colored

sand into a glass container, a visual reminder that what was once separate is now combined forever.

- Eucharist
- Blessing or Benediction
- Presentation of the Couple: The officiant presents to the congregation, Mr. and Mrs. John Smith. The congregation applauds. If the bride will be keeping her maiden name, the clergy will present Mr. John Smith and his wife, Mary Jones.
- The ceremony is now over, and the wedding party leaves in the recessional, followed by the guests.

Parts of the Ceremony (Jewish)

- After the wedding party is assembled under the chuppah, the ceremony begins with the Blessing: "Blessed may you be who come in the name of the Lord ..."
- Address or Prayer
- Blessing of the Bride and Groom: The rabbi presents a cup of wine to the groom and then to the bride.
- Groom's Vows "Do you take this woman ...?"
- Bride's Vows: "Do you take this man ...?"
- The Rings
- The Ketubah is read
- The Seven Blessings: The wine is passed once more to the groom, then to the bride.
- Pronouncement
- Blessing
- Breaking of the Glass
- The guests all shout "Mazel Tov!" and the recessional begins, followed by the guests.

The Recessional

The recessional is led by you and your groom. You are on your new husband's right, either on his arm or holding his hand. The best man will escort the maid of honor, and the ushers will escort the bridesmaids.

The parents of the bride and groom follow. The pews empty out from front to back.

The Jewish recessional is also led by the bride and groom, with the bride on the groom's left. This time, they are followed by the bride's parents, the groom's parents, the best man with the maid of honor, the rabbi with the cantor, and finally the ushers escorting the bridesmaids.

The lineup of the Christian and Jewish recessionals follows on the next two pages.

Examples of Recessionals

Example 1

Example of a Christian recessional

Bride/Groom
Flower Girl/Ring Bearer
Maid of Honor/Best Man
Bridesmaid/Usher
Bridesmaid/Usher
Bridesmaid/Usher

Example 2

Example of a Jewish recessional

Groom/Bride
Father of Bride/Mother of Bride
Father of Groom/Mother of Groom
Best Man/Maid of Honor
Rabbi/Cantor
Usher/Bridesmaid
Usher/Bridesmaid
Usher/Bridesmaid
Usher/Bridesmaid

After the Ceremony

The receiving line can be formed immediately after the ceremony, in the foyer of the church, although this is usually done upon arrival at the reception site. If you decide to have the receiving line now, there will not be another later, unless there are few guests invited to the ceremony and many to the reception.

This is also a time for photographs. Often, the wedding party moves to a garden setting for this purpose. All cities have parks that can be used, or you may wish to have a historical building and its grounds as a backdrop.

If he has not already done so, the best man will deliver the clergy's fee, as well as a cash gift to anyone who has helped out at the wedding.

The cars or limousines will be lined up to take the wedding party to the reception. As you make your way to the car, guests will shower you with rose petals, birdseed, or potpourri; all of these are alternatives to confetti. Check with the clergy ahead of time to see what is allowed. Many do not like birdseed because the birds leave droppings. They might permit grass seed.

Bubbles are popular, but don't try to cut costs by using liquid soap or children's bubbles. Anything but real wedding bubbles will stain delicate wedding fabrics.

Some brides like the idea of having each guest ring a tiny bell. These make a lovely keepsake, but do not hand them out until the very last moment or you will hear a lot of extra sound on the wedding video!

Have a butterfly or dove release. Be warned, though, that under certain circumstances, the doves or butterflies can be lethargic and not fly.

More Ideas

- Use many candles to symbolize God's presence. Put them on an altar or behind the chuppah.
- In a Christian ceremony, have the clergy and both families enter in a single procession. This will symbolize the uniting of the two families and their support for the couple.
- Have a hymn sung by a boys' choir.

- Honor couples who have been married a long time.
- After the reception, donate the flowers to a local hospital.
- Use a chuppah that is a family heirloom. Have your initials and wedding date embroidered along the edge.
- Before breaking the glass, wrap it in an heirloom handkerchief, embroidered with your names and date. Buy a set of glasses and break the first one, saving the rest for future family weddings.
- Plant lilies after the wedding, in the Dutch tradition. Their yearly blooming symbolizes renewal.
- Have a processional played on a single trumpet. The *Trumpet Voluntary* is the perfect choice.
- Plant a tree on the church grounds.
- Have a snapshot taken, Hollywood style, of each guest arriving for the ceremony. When you send the thank-you notes, enclose a picture of the guest "walking the red carpet."

Ceremony Site Checklist

What are the religious requirements?

Can the bride and groom write their own vows?

What is the officiant's fee?

What is the organist's fee?

Is there a dressing room for bride and bridesmaids?

Is premarital counseling mandatory?

Are aisle runners, candles, etc., included?

Is there adequate parking?

Is there wheelchair access?

What are the restrictions on music?

What are the restrictions on photography and videography?

What are the restrictions on confetti, birdseed, etc.?

How many guests will the church/venue hold?

Ceremony Wording Worksheet

(CHRISTIAN)

Use this worksheet as you plan the ceremony, to make notes, record names of soloists and readers, etc.

CALL TO WORSHIP:

PRAYER:

SCRIPTURE READING:

MEDITATION:

DECLARATION OF CONSENT:

ADDITIONAL PRAYERS OR READINGS:

BRIDE'S VOWS:

GROOM'S VOWS:

BLESSING AND EXCHANGE OF RINGS:

PRONOUNCEMENT:

PRAYER:

SOLOIST:

UNITY CANDLE:

BLESSING OR BENEDICTION:

PRESENTATION OF THE COUPLE:

PRESENTATION OF THE ROSES:

Ceremony Wording Worksheet

(JEWISH)

Use this worksheet as you plan the ceremony, to make notes, record names of soloists and readers, etc.

BLESSING:

ADDRESS OR PRAYER:

BLESSING OF THE BRIDE AND GROOM:

GROOM'S VOWS:

BRIDE'S VOWS:

RINGS:

KETUBAH:

SEVEN BLESSINGS:

PRONOUNCEMENT:

BLESSING:

BREAKING OF THE GLASS:

PRESENTATION OF THE ROSES:

For Your Notes

CHAPTER 13

The Reception

Types and Styles of Receptions

The type of wedding reception will determine many of the other details. Let the location and formality of the ceremony guide you.

As a general rule, the later the reception begins the more formal it will be. However, this doesn't always hold true. Wedding breakfasts (a tradition of the Royal Family) are very formal.

The wedding breakfast follows a morning wedding and is held before one o'clock in the afternoon. A lighter meal is served, and wedding cake is a must. Alcoholic beverages are not served, although champagne is provided for toasting. The meal is usually in the form of a light buffet, including quiche, strawberries, and crepes. For a midday reception, add salads, cold poached salmon, and pasta to the above.

Afternoon tea is held from two o'clock to five o'clock in the afternoon. Sandwiches, hors d'oeuvres, and wedding cake are served. Alcoholic beverages are permissible, and punch is a must.

A cocktail reception is similar to the afternoon tea, but is held later in the day and offers a wider choice of alcoholic beverages.

An evening reception includes a cocktail hour, followed by a sit-down dinner or a buffet. Station buffets are quite popular. Each station is a buffet of foods with a specific theme, such as Mediterranean or Oriental. Several stations placed around the room offer guests a choice.

After eight, a dessert reception can be held. As well as wedding cake, there will be a sweet table. A full bar is not appropriate, but brandy and specialty coffees can be served.

Another later reception is the champagne reception, where champagne is the only alcoholic beverage offered. Cocktail sandwiches, hors d'oeuvres, and wedding cake are served.

Reception Venues

One of your first decisions will be the location of your wedding reception. Often, the ceremony and reception can be held at the same location, cutting down on travel and creating opportunities for creativity. This is only possible for Roman Catholic ceremonies, however, if the church has a hall that can be used for wedding receptions. The cost is reasonable for a couple on a budget, and any equipment lacking can be easily rented.

Receptions after a home wedding can be simple or formal, in keeping with the size and style of your home.

Some reception halls offer a small chapel for the wedding ceremony. They use their own caterers, and many provide additional services such as flowers, cakes, and even invitations. Some of these facilities host several receptions at the same time. Check such details as sound transference, privacy, and parking. Visit during an actual wedding, but be inconspicuous.

Country clubs and hotels offer first-class meals and stunning decor. As a rule, you will get the most professional service from this type of location. In the case of a golf and country club, find out ahead of time about the policy regarding rentals to nonmembers.

Many associations have large halls that are available to rent when not in use for their own functions. They have kitchen facilities and plenty of room. The decor is usually very plain, requiring extensive decorating. Again, check nonmember policies.

Some restaurants are reluctant to close to the public in order to host a private reception; others will do so outside their peak operating hours. An intimate reception is another matter. Many restaurants have private rooms that can be used for smaller groups.

In many large cities with harbors, you can rent a boat for a wedding on the water, with the city lights in the background and romantic strolls on the deck. Some charge a site fee; others charge per plate.

Almost every area has mansions, castles, mills, or museums that are available for receptions. In some cases, you must use the in-house caterer. Ask about the rules involving candles, electrical equipment, confetti, and restricted areas.

With all these choices, you would think that booking a reception venue would be easy. However, the locations that are clearly superior will sometimes be booked more than a year ahead.

When I am hired to help a couple find the perfect location, I eliminate many ahead of time and show them the three best choices. I suggest you do the same: look at the brochures, and then go to see your three favorites.

Caterers

If you will be using an in-house (on-premise) caterer, the staff at the reception venue will work with you on such details as the menu and the bar, as well as linens and china.

If you need to hire an independent caterer, there is much more planning involved. Anything that the caterer does not provide must be rented.

When weighing your options, be aware that costs can unintentionally become inflated. For example, it is a well-known fact that a buffet costs less than a sit-down dinner. However, the tables need to be decorated and more food is needed because many guests go back for seconds; you can easily see your savings evaporate.

Work out the wait-staff ratio–the ratio of staff to guests. It will be determined by the style of service. Plated service usually uses one waiter for two tables. Based on tables of eight to ten people, each waiter will look after sixteen to twenty guests.

Find out what happens to the dirty dishes. The caterer will usually take them away and wash them at their headquarters.

Types of Service

The most common types of service at a wedding reception are plated service and buffet service. Plated service is sometimes called American service. The plates are brought in from the kitchen on large trays and served by the wait staff. Buffet service allows the guests to serve themselves from long tables upon which the food is displayed. Other types of service, less commonly seen, may prove suitable for your wedding reception.

- French service is when the dish is prepared at the table while the guests watch. You have no doubt seen this done in restaurants, usually with a flambé dish. For the average wedding reception, though, it is usually cost-prohibitive.
- Cocktail service involves trays of hors d'oeuvres and champagne, served by waiters who circulate around the guests.
- Russian service, also called silver service, has the guests serving themselves from trays held by the waiter.
- Food stations are becoming quite popular. The service is similar to that of a buffet, but each station is situated in a different area of the room, so the long lineups are not a problem. Each station has its own chef, and the food served in each reflects a certain theme, such as Mediterranean, Italian, or vegetarian.
- Hand service is the most labor-intensive. It is used only at the most formal receptions. Each waiter serves only two guests. When all the waiters are beside the guests they will be serving, the maitre d' gives the signal to serve the plates simultaneously. If warming covers are used, a second signal prompts their removal.

Compare the types of service to determine the best for your own circumstances. The more labor-intensive types will be more expensive.

The Menu

Whether you will be working with an in-house caterer or an independent outside caterer, they will advise you on the selection of the menu.

Most caterers will set up a special luncheon for you and your fiancé, called a "tasting appointment," where you will sample items from the menu. From there you can make your selections.

The menu will be determined by the type of reception you will be having. The sit-down dinner is the most formal, and the buffet is increasingly popular. The cocktail reception offers sophistication, and the afternoon tea is a return to yesteryear. Collect menus from various caterers in your area, and then leisurely contemplate your choice.

The caterer must note any food allergies in writing. Nut allergies, which are often fatal, are becoming more and more common. Some people are also allergic to latex, making it necessary for the caterer to wear another type of glove.

The caterer can prepare a special meal for any guest needing a sodium reduced, lactose intolerant, diabetic, vegan, or vegetarian meal.

The popularity of the buffet is due in part to the fact that you are offering your guests a choice. Two or three hot dishes (offering a choice between meat and poultry), two or three salads for variety, a selection of rolls or bread, and a selection of vegetables, and dessert should be more than enough.

Even at a sit-down dinner, it has become common to offer guests a choice of entree. You will recall from Chapter 5 that some reply cards require the guest to check their preference. It is not necessary to elaborate; simply "beef" or "chicken" will suffice.

Tents

If your wedding is to take place during the summer, a rented tent will solve your space problems. Your rental company will advise you on the size and style. Many options are available, including lighting and temperature control.

Tents are available in colors, but white is the most elegant and is the one recommended for weddings. Features such as French doors and Palladian windows add to the ambiance.

Tents can be erected on just about any surface, but the area must be free from sprinklers, underground wires, and cables. Grassy areas are best, but never erect a tent on freshly cut grass. Choose your flooring accordingly. The choices run the gamut from wood parquet to carpeting, and everything in between.

Ask if the tent rental company will have someone from their staff on-site the day of your wedding to handle any problems that arise.

I often recommend a second, open-sided tent in which to place the DJ, or to allow guests to sit in the fresh air. Rented portable toilets should be placed a reasonable distance from the tent for convenience.

Your tent rental company will work out the ideal size. As general guideline, use the following formula: For each guest, allow 12 square feet.

Extra space is needed for buffet tables. For every 75 guests, allow one buffet table. According to these calculations, 100 guests need 1200 square feet of space, which calls for a 30 foot x 40 foot tent. Some rental companies recommend 10 square feet per person, but I find that it is better to err on the generous side.

Rentals

No rental company can provide *everything* you could never wish for; you should visit several. Here are just a few of the items available for rent:

- Tents
- Tables and chairs
- Linens
- Punch bowls
- Silver, china, and crystal
- Silver serving pieces
- Arches
- Wishing wells
- Candle stands
- Fountains
- Potted trees and topiaries
- Portable bars
- Portable washrooms
- Candelabra
- Centerpieces
- Dance floors
- Gazebos

Calculate the number of guests before contacting the rental company, in order to get an accurate estimate.

Portable washrooms are no longer like the ones we see on construction sites. They are clean and beautiful, with sinks, running water, towels, and even floral decorations.

The Head Table

The head table we see most often consists of the bride and groom with their wedding party, and is situated against the main wall of the room. Often the table is placed on a riser, so that the guests can more easily see the wedding party. Do not use a riser if any member of the wedding party will experience difficulty with the step.

Many couples want to be better able to converse with their wedding party during dinner. In this case, the head table can be a round table, located in a special area of the room and set apart with a special centerpiece.

You will be seated at the right of your groom. The best man sits beside you and the maid of honor sits beside your groom. To either side, the bridesmaids and ushers alternate. The ring bearer and flower girl sit with their own parents. If they are your children, they usually sit with a friend or relative, although they can sit with you at the head table if you wish.

A larger head table can be horseshoe-shaped, and will often include the parents. Most often, though, the parents are seated at a different table, together with the grandparents and perhaps the siblings. If the siblings have friends at the wedding, they may choose to sit with them. The clergy and their spouse are seated at the parents' table. If the parents are at the head table, seat the clergy with grandparents or distinguished relatives.

If your parents are divorced and remarried, the second husband or wife must be seated with their spouse. If there is animosity in the family, have two separate parent tables. Under no circumstances are you to seat divorced parents together with the second spouse elsewhere.

Spouses and dates of the wedding party are seated together at a special table. However, if they have other friends attending, they may prefer to be with them.

Balloons

Although it is considered improper to have balloons in a church wedding and equally improper to use balloons to decorate an ultra-formal reception venue, there are times when balloons can be used at a less formal reception to add just the right touch of festivity.

Dollar-for-dollar, balloons let you fill up space, brighten dark rooms, and add splashes of color like nothing else can.

As with any other aspect of your wedding, you will want to avoid the amateurs. A certified balloon artist is entitled to use the initials CBA.

Avoid clichés, such as hearts with doves in the center. Think of some different ways to use balloons. For example:

- Place a balloon arch at the entrance to the hall, and have guests enter through it.
- Three helium-filled balloons, tied with ribbons and attached to weights, make a festive centerpiece for each table. Be sure that the balloons are high enough so as not to make conversation difficult.
- Clear balloons are especially romantic.
- Balloons can be used to make an enchanting canopy over the dance floor.

The Master of Ceremonies

Although it is possible to hire a Master of Ceremonies (or Mistress of Ceremonies) from a speaker's group, you will most likely want to give that job to a special friend or family member.

The main duty of the MC is to introduce the head table and coordinate the speeches. In addition, the MC draws attention to the buffet tables and the order in which the guests are to proceed and announces the gathering of the guests for the throwing of the bouquet and garter, the cake cutting, and the bride and groom's last dance.

To introduce the head table, the MC must do a little advance research. He will have already made notes with the person's name, their relationship to the two of you, and their role in the wedding. Preview the jokes and anecdotes to be sure they are tasteful. The successful MC will always be careful never to embarrass, and will follow a humorous comment with a positive one. Each introduction is best kept to sixty seconds or less.

It is absolutely necessary that you provide your MC with a timeline of the wedding reception, a seating plan for the head table, and the correct pronunciation of the names. If any names are difficult to pronounce, spell them out phonetically.

Champagne

Champagne was invented by accident when a French monk discovered that some wine he had made was full of gas bubbles. To this day, one of the most exquisite champagnes bears his name: *Dom Perignon*.

The vineyards attended by Dom Perignon were in Champagne, in Northeastern France, a district that has given its name to the unique wines produced here. Only recently have other sparkling wines made with the same method been permitted to call themselves champagne.

Vintage champagnes are made from a single harvest of grapes and aged for at least three years. 80 percent of the market is made up of non-vintage champagnes, which are a blend of the current year's harvest with up to forty *reserve wines*. This produces a consistent blend, whatever the year. The ultimate, and most expensive, is a *Prestige Cuvée*, which is aged much longer.

White, red, and black grapes are used to make the champagne. Individual brands of champagne use different portions of the blend, with pink champagne deriving its color from black grapes.

The driest champagne is known as *brut* and those which are slightly sweet are called *demi sec*. Italian sparkling wines are known as *spumante* (dry) and *asti spumante* (sweet).

Dom Perignon is quoted as saying that the bubbles in champagne made it "like drinking stars." The better the champagne, the smaller the bubbles. They are captured by the tulip shape of the champagne flute.

Champagne should be well-chilled after thirty minutes in ice water or twenty-four hours in the refrigerator. The cork will stick or shrink if it is chilled any longer than this.

Although Prestige Cuvée or vintage champagnes may occasionally be harder to find, there is no truth to the rumors that there is a champagne shortage. There are presently one billion bottles of champagne in vineyard cellars.

The Bar

Most wedding receptions involve the serving of alcoholic beverages. Some have only a champagne toast, some have a full bar of wine, beer, and liquor, and others are somewhere in between.

Many reception venues handle the bar themselves. They are licensed under their local laws, and they provide both the alcohol and the bartender. If you are planning a wedding in a historic location or at home, you must take care of these details yourselves. The laws vary with each location. In most areas, you are required to have a permit and the bartenders you hire must have undergone special training. Many bars and restaurants will give you the names of their bartenders who are not working on the night of your wedding. The bartender will refuse to serve anyone who is obviously inebriated. Alternatively, he can alert you so that you can approach the guest yourself and offer to call a taxi.

When deciding how much to buy, keep in mind that if you do not open the bottles, they can be returned. It is better to err on the generous side. You know your friends and family; you know what they drink and how much. Begin with a few figures:

- The average 26 oz / 750 ml bottle of wine will serve 5
- The average champagne bottle will serve 6 in flutes
- A case of champagne will allow 72 people to toast
- A 26 oz / 750 ml bottle of liquor will provide 17 (1 oz) drinks
- A 40 oz / 1.14 litre bottle of liquor will provide 25 (1 oz) drinks
- For each bottle of liquor, plan on three bottles of mix
- The average wedding guest will have four drinks during the evening
- To get 100 drinks, you need 100 bottles of beer, 6 bottles (750 ml) of liquor, or 20 bottles (750 ml) of wine
- To estimate wine for dinner, allow 2 glasses per person

Use the number of guests to estimate your needs. For beer, divide the guest list in half and then multiply by the number of hours the reception will last. For liquor, divide the list by four, multiply by the number of hours, and then divide by the number of options (rye, gin, vodka, etc.)

To serve twenty, have a punch made from one bottle of liquor and twelve cups of juice. A nonalcoholic punch is also needed.

Mixes include tonic or soda water, cola, ginger ale, lemon-lime, and fruit juices. Stock plenty of soft drinks, juice, and water for designated drivers and non-drinkers. Have ginger ale or a nonalcoholic sparkling wine for those who wish to toast the couple without champagne.

Stock the bar with the following:

- Ice: allow just over one pound per person
- Garnishes: include olives, orange slices, and maraschino cherries
- Seasonings: Tabasco sauce, Worcestershire sauce, salt

Finally, you need bar equipment. You probably own some of these items; the rest can be acquired inexpensively.

- Glasses: wine glasses, champagne flutes, highballs, old-fashioned, Martini
- Ice bucket and tongs
- Toothpicks
- Long spoon for stirring
- Cocktail shaker
- Bottle opener
- Corkscrew
- Knife and cutting board
- Shot glasses
- Napkins, straws

The Wedding Cake

Set on its own table and cut as part of the festivities, the wedding cake is the showpiece of the reception. Wedding cakes can be made in any flavor and can be iced in any color, although white or off-white icing is most often seen.

Most bakeries will allow you to sample their products. You have a choice of flavor for the cake itself and another for the filling. They are all so irresistible that many couples order a different flavor for each layer!

You may wish to decorate the cake with real flowers. In this case, the cake is ordered with plain icing and the florist will place the flowers on-site.

Cake layers can be separated by pillars or placed directly on top of one another. The topper is a special part of the cake and will become a keepsake for years to come.

When the cake is delivered to the reception venue, have someone inspect it according to the order specifications and request any necessary touchups to the icing. Have the cake set up on a special table with a silver cake knife and server. Many brides purchase them as a set and have them engraved with the wedding date.

The *Groom's cake* is traditionally a fruitcake. It is packaged in small boxes or wrapped in foil and a paper doily, and given to the guests to take home. The Groom's cake is optional; many couples choose to forego this tradition.

Favors

It is correct to give a favor to each guest, although you will often see one for each couple. Many of these ideas are quite inexpensive. Some are handmade, which makes them even more special!

- Votive candleholders of any description. Dress them up with tulle and ribbon
- Small decorative flowerpots, holding place cards, with a packet of seeds
- Mini-bottles of wine or champagne, with your names and wedding date on the label
- Miniature straw hats decorated with silk flowers and ribbon
- Paper fans, perhaps with the name of the guest in calligraphy
- Miniature gift boxes, filled with candy, almonds, or any other treat
- Miniature picture frames, perhaps with the name of the guest in calligraphy
- A CD of your favorite love songs
- A single red rose
- A romantic tree ornament for a Christmas wedding

- Homemade cookies in the shape of a heart
- An evergreen seedling in a burlap bag

Some couples choose to forgo the favors, and place a framed notice on the table to let guests know that a donation has been made to charity in their honor.

Italian weddings are known for "confetti" (sugared almonds). The bitter almond and the sweet sugar symbolize the bitter-sweetness of marriage. There is always an odd number, meaning good luck.

The Bride and Groom Arrive

One of the grandest moments of the reception is the first appearance of the bride and groom. The wedding is over, and you are now ready to enjoy your first big celebration as husband and wife. It is perhaps the largest party that will ever be held in your honor!

Most of the guests will be assembled ahead of time to greet you. It is at this time that they will sign the guest book. Place the book near the entrance to the hall with a plume pen beside it, perhaps the same pen you used to sign the register during the ceremony.

An alternative idea, one that will create an heirloom, is to have a silver tray and an engraving pen for the guests to sign. Or, have your guests sign a picture matte, which you will use to frame your favorite wedding picture.

The Receiving Line

If the receiving line was not held at the church, it will form immediately upon arrival at the reception. The line can form from the right or left, depending on the space, but the order in which the guests greet the wedding party and parents is always the same.

The flower girl and ring bearer are not expected to participate. Sometimes, the fathers of the bride and groom decide not to be in the line; in this case, they will mingle and greet the guests. The order of the receiving line is as follows:

- Mother of the bride
- Father of the bride
- Mother of the groom
- Father of the groom
- Maid of honor
- Bride
- Groom
- Best man
- Bridesmaids and ushers alternating

If the women are wearing hats and gloves, they will leave them on. If there are many guests, the receiving line will be quite long; provide refreshments for those who are waiting. Greetings should be brief; you can always visit later.

At a very small, informal wedding, you can eliminate the receiving line, as long as you make a point of stopping and talking with each guest. For a formal wedding, the receiving line is a must.

When introducing two people, etiquette demands that the older person is addressed first, such as "Aunt Betty, I'd like you to meet my husband William."

To calculate the time needed for the receiving line, consider that each guest takes approximately twenty seconds. Therefore, a receiving line with 150 guests will take approximately fifty minutes.

The Guests are Seated

Near the entrance, guests will locate their place cards to find their assigned table. The tables are numbered, and each place card will have a corresponding number. Some brides prefer not to use place cards, setting up an easel near the entrance to the room instead. Guests find their names listed table-by-table.

When the guests are seated, the wedding party is ready to enter the room and make their way to the head table. The Master or Mistress of Ceremonies will take the microphone as the bridal party lines up in order just outside the door. Bridesmaids are paired with ushers and the maid of honor with the best man, just as they were for the recessional. The MC will announce each person by name and by their position in the wedding party, as they enter and take their place at the head table. Finally, the MC will announce you, the new husband and wife, to the applause of your guests!

Speeches and Toasts

All weddings, no matter how small or informal, have time set aside for toasts and speeches.

The best man proposes the first toast to you and your new husband. He will share an anecdote of a past experience he and the groom have shared, but he must be careful to avoid any risqué topics or references to former girlfriends. Have your groom read over the best man's speech, just to be sure that there is nothing embarrassing in it.

This is followed by the groom's toast to you, the bride. In his speech, he will praise your best features and thank your parents for raising such a wonderful young woman. He will finish by thanking his own parents.

The maid of honor will propose the next toast to the newlyweds. Her speech will also share an amusing story.

After this toast, other speeches and toasts may be offered, by your father, your mother, or even you. These are not mandatory.

The subjects of a toast do not raise their glasses, nor do they take a sip. When the guests stand to drink the toast, you and your groom remain seated.

Speeches can be humorous or emotional (or a little of both), but they must be short. Anything longer than three minutes should be edited. Notes are okay, but the speech should be rehearsed so that the notes are there just for a reminder. Anyone who will be proposing a toast should be careful not to drink too much beforehand. The combination of alcohol and stage fright will not make a successful speaker. If you will be speaking, remember to speak slowly and not fidget. Trembling hands should be gently clasped and rested on the podium.

A word about kissing games–they accomplish nothing except interrupting the first meal that the bride and groom have had all day. If you both like them, go ahead. Otherwise, spread the word that you might prefer an alternative, such as having the guests recite a love poem in exchange for a chance to see you kiss.

Cutting the Wedding Cake

You and your groom make the first cut. Next, you cut a piece for both of you, symbolizing your traditional role. In another symbolic gesture, your new husband feeds the first bite to you. As a symbol of respect and thanks, you can both serve their parents if you wish.

After the pictures have been taken, the cake is removed and cut in the kitchen. Sometimes, the kitchen staff is given a sheet cake to cut, and the tiered cake cut by the bride and groom is actually a model with one real layer. If the entire cake is real, a waiter may cut it in the reception hall, while the guests line up buffet-style at his table. At a very small wedding, you may decide to cut the cake yourselves, allowing you another opportunity to chat with each guest individually. Practice well beforehand!

At a formal sit-down dinner, the cake is cut and served shortly after the meal, forming part of the dessert. At an informal buffet dinner, it is cut a little later.

Many couples freeze the top tier of their wedding cake to enjoy on their first anniversary. If you plan to do this, be sure to seal it properly. Otherwise, you may find that a year later it will taste like freezer burn!

Throwing the Bouquet and Garter

The throwing of the garter and bouquet are popular with the guests who participate in these rituals. The groom removes the bride's garter, to the shouts and whistles of the male guests. He then tosses it to the single men in the crowd as they scramble to catch it.

Some feel that this practice has no place in a wedding; others don't mind it at all. Undignified though it may seem, it's just harmless fun. If you want to include it in your wedding, by all means go ahead. The garter should be moved to just below your knee.

As you throw the bouquet to all single women in the room you may wish to aim at your sister or a special friend, but most brides toss the bouquet over the shoulder.

According to tradition, those who catch the bouquet and garter will be the next to marry. Often, the woman who catches the bouquet and the man who catches the garter will share a dance. If you want to have this custom at your wedding, advise the DJ ahead of time, so that he can select a song.

The Bride and Groom Depart

Recently, we have seen a change in how and when the bride and groom leave their wedding reception.

Traditionally, the bride tossed her bouquet, the groom tossed the garter, and the couple changed into their going-away outfits. Then, they said their good-byes and left in a shower of rice or confetti.

Today, the bride and groom are reluctant to leave the reception and are there to say good-bye as their guests depart. Let the guests know if you will be staying until the reception is over. Many, especially older people, will be familiar with the old tradition that considered it impolite to leave before the bride and groom.

If you plan a dramatic getaway, find out the facility's policies regarding confetti. Most forbid it, and will charge hefty cleanup fees to those who ignore the rule. There are, however, many alternatives:

- Have the guests wave sparklers.
- Have the guests stand in two lines and join hands, forming an arch for the two of you to run through.
- Have each guest throw birdseed, grass seed, or rose petals. Again, you must check the rules; many of these are also forbidden.
- Have the guests ring tiny bells, which they can keep as favors.
- Have the guests blow bubbles. Use a bubble solution made for weddings. Anything else will stain delicate fabrics.

While all of these options are fun, keep in mind that it is not necessary to have the guests do anything but take pictures as you leave for your honeymoon.

Reception Site Checklist

What is the rental fee?

Parking?

Fee?

Ceremony and reception?

China, silver, and glassware included?

Linens included?

Tables and chairs included?

In-house caterer?

Piano?

Music restrictions?

Adequate electrical outlets?

Kitchen facilities?

Dance floor?

Wheelchair access?

Dressing rooms for bride and groom?

Microphone and podium?

Coat check?

Fee?

Existing bar, or must you buy your own liquor under special permit?

NOTES

Reception Menu Worksheet

Punch and hors d'oeuvres upon arrival

Wine on tables

Champagne

Appetizers

Bread and/or rolls

Soup/salad

Main course

Desserts

Coffee, tea, specialty coffees

Late-night sweet table

Reception Seating Worksheet

Table #

Table #

Table #

Table #

Table #

Table #

Floor Plan of the Reception Area

Use this page to create a scaled floor plan of the reception hall. As well as the head table, include tables for the guests, the DJ, the cake, and the gifts. Indicate the dance floor and bar. Show all windows, doors, and other architectural features of the room.

For Your Notes

CHAPTER 14

Cultural and Religious Weddings

The Christian Wedding Ceremony

The three main Christian wedding ceremonies are Catholic, Protestant, and Orthodox. There are approximately nine hundred Protestant denominations worldwide. The similarities will be presented in this chapter. As well, we will look at Mormon and Quaker ceremonies as an example of the wide variety within the Christian faith.

Saturday is the most common day of the week for a Christian wedding. Although Sunday weddings can be held, Sunday is not a popular wedding day, simply because the church and clergy are most busy on that day. A Catholic wedding without Mass can be held before noon. A wedding with Mass can be held in the morning or afternoon, but never after six o'clock in the evening. The Nuptial Mass, the most traditional Catholic ceremony, takes place at high noon. During Lent the wedding will be very simple.

Protestant

A Protestant wedding can be held at any location. If a particular minister does not do weddings outside the church, he will recommend one who does. The ceremony consists of many elements, although they vary from church to church. Central to the Protestant wedding service is the comparison of Christ's relationship with His church to a man's relationship with his wife. After the organ prelude, the wedding party enters the church in a processional. When they have assembled at the altar, the clergy will address the congregation. He/she will ask for anyone who knows a reason the couple should not be married to come forward, and will ask the couple themselves to declare any such reason. This is followed by the "Statement of Intent." A Scripture reading is followed by a short sermon, or homily. The bride and groom exchange vows and rings, after which they are pronounced husband and wife. Several prayers, including the Lord's Prayer, follow and the couple signs the marriage register. They then lead the recessional out of the church.

The Protestant bride is given away by her father. If her stepfather raised her in the absence of her natural father, he may do the honors. If the bride has had a relationship with her natural father he should fill this role, even if she has lived with her mother and stepfather. After he has escorted the bride up the aisle, her father will respond to the officiant's question of "Who gives this woman to be married to this man?" by saying "I do." Sometimes both parents answer "We do," the mother of the bride speaking from her place in the front pew. If the bride is older, or if she has been married before, this part of the ceremony is often omitted.

Protestant weddings place a special importance on candlelight. The unity candle is often part of the service. Two candles are lit before the ceremony by the bride and groom or by their mothers, and the center candle is lit from these at the appropriate time in the service, symbolizing that two separate lives have become one. Sometimes the two side candles are snuffed, but many couples like to leave them lit as a symbol that they are still individuals.

Catholic

The Catholic ceremony with Mass *must* take place inside a church, as it is considered to be one of the seven sacraments. It is often performed in conjunction with the sacrament of reconciliation (confession) and the sacrament of the Eucharist (communion) as in the Nuptial Mass.

Many of the elements present in the Protestant ceremony, such as the unity candle, are present. There are, however, some differences. Although the bride is escorted up the aisle by her father, he does not give her away.

For three consecutive weeks before the wedding, the banns are published in the church bulletin, or the priest can read them during Mass.

As a rule, this is done only if the bride and groom are both Catholic. Banns are published in all parishes in which the bride has lived for more than six months since the age of twelve, and the groom since the age of fourteen.

The Catholic bride will often place her bouquet at a statue of the Blessed Virgin Mary.

Orthodox

The Orthodox ceremony is quite different than the Protestant and Catholic services. There is an emphasis on the number three, signifying the Trinity. The Betrothal Ceremony comes first. The wedding party is met by the priest at the door of the church, where the bride and groom confirm that they have come of their own free will to be married. He then invites them to stand at the altar. After blessing the rings, the priest places them on the right hands of the couple. The best man exchanges the rings between the bride and the groom three times. Throughout the Sacrament of Holy Matrimony, the bride and groom hold lighted candles. There is a reference to couples in the Old Testament, as well as a series of petitions and prayers.

The Matrimonial Coronation is the climax of the Eastern Orthodox wedding ceremony. The priest or the best man places two ornate crowns on the heads of the bride and groom. The crowns are connected by a ribbon that ties the bride and groom for the rest of the ceremony, and indeed, for the rest of their lives. The priest prays that God will bless the couple by crowning them with honor and glory. While the bride and groom hold hands, the priest moves the crowns back and forth on the couple's heads, exchanging them three times.

The bride and groom drink from a single cup of red wine, and the priest leads them around the altar three times, in a circle that has no end. After the final prayers and blessing, the priest separates their hands with a Bible, showing that only God can come between them.

As in a Catholic wedding, the Orthodox bride often places her flowers at the altar of the Blessed Virgin Mary.

The crowns are often displayed at the reception. They can be made locally or imported from Greece. Traditionally, the best man chose the crowns, but today the bride and groom choose their own, in keeping with the style of the wedding. An Eastern Orthodox Church in your area will give you the name of a local crown maker.

Mormon (Church of Latter-Day Saints)

There are two different types of Mormon weddings: the standard church ceremony and the temple ceremony.

The standard ceremony is open to any Mormon, and can be officiated by the couple's local bishop.

The temple wedding requires a *sealing ordinance*. To obtain this, the couple sets up a meeting with their local bishop to answer various questions regarding their beliefs and their lifestyle. If the bishop is satisfied that they are following of the laws of the church, he will sign a *temple recommend*. This will be taken to the *stake president*, who will ask many of the same questions and add his signature to the *temple recommend*.

The temple ceremony will be held at one of the worldwide Mormon temples. Family and friends must also have a *temple recommend* if they are to attend. It will be officiated by the *temple sealer* in front of two witnesses. In all other ways, the ceremony is similar to that of any Protestant faith.

The most distinguishing feature of the Mormon temple wedding is that the couple marries in this life and in the afterlife. The vows do not say, "until death do us part," but rather "for time and all eternity."

If a couple marries in a civil ceremony or a standard wedding ceremony, they can later have a second ceremony to seal the marriage for eternity.

Quaker

The Quakers believe that only God can marry a couple; therefore, they do not require an officiant at the wedding. Instead, the couple must write a letter of intent, which will be read and discussed by members of the *clearness committee*.

This committee does not take its responsibilities lightly; its two or three members discuss the couple and any issues that may be present. They report their decision at the next monthly business meeting. Upon acceptance, the *clearness committee* will appoint an *oversight committee*, which does the same work as a wedding planner. The committee reserves a meeting house, handles the legalities (a valid marriage license is still required), and plans the reception.

The ceremony itself takes place during a weekly worship meeting. After silent worship, the bride and groom stand and hold hands. Their vows are simple: "In the presence of God and before these our families and friends, I take thee (name) to be my husband/wife as long as we both shall live." After the newlyweds sign the marriage certificate, all present sign it as witnesses. A friend or relative reads it aloud, and the worship service continues.

The Jewish Wedding Ceremony

The Jewish faith is divided into three groups: Orthodox, Conservative, and Reform. The Orthodox movement is the oldest and follows the *Torah* literally. The Reform movement began in the late 1800s in Germany and is the most liberal. The Conservative movement follows the middle of the road.

Their wedding day is considered a personal *Yom Kippur* for the bride and groom, for on this day all their past sins are forgiven as they merge into a new soul.

Jewish weddings are not performed on the Sabbath (Friday sundown to Saturday sundown), *Rosh Hashanah*, *Passover*, *Sukkot*, *Yom Kippur*, or *Shavout*. The time of day is optional; the later the hour, the more formal the wedding.

Most Jewish wedding ceremonies are performed in synagogues, but can be held anywhere a *chuppah* is raised. This is a canopy on four poles, which represents the couple's new home. It is open on all sides in honor of Abraham, who had doors on all sides of his home as a symbol of hospitality. The *chuppah* can have stationary poles set up before the ceremony, or it can be part of the processional, using four honored pole bearers.

Yarmulkes must be worn by all male guests, even gentile friends. They can be ordered in many colors and embroidered with the wedding date and the names of the bride and the groom.

Conservative and Orthodox grooms read from the *Torah* on the Sabbath before the wedding. If a Conservative bride knows Hebrew she can join him, but an Orthodox woman never reads from the *Torah*.

Since the first century, the *ketubah* is a legal contract, signed by the groom and two unrelated Jewish males. It outlines the groom's responsibilities to the bride. During the ceremony, the *ketubah* is read and presented to the bride. It is common to have an artist design a *ketubah* that the couple can hang in their home.

All three groups place a special significance on the wedding ring. Traditionally, there must be an act of *kinyan,* the physical "buying" of the bride, in which the groom presents the bride with an object of nominal value. Since the seventh century this has been a ring, placed on the index finger to the second knuckle; it is thought that this finger leads to the soul. The ring must be of gold with no precious stones. If the bride would rather have a ring set with diamonds, the groom can have one blessed and present it to her after the ceremony.

The parents of the bride and groom take part in the processional and the recessional, and they stand with the couple under the *chuppah.* The attendants stand outside the *chuppah.*

Many brides continue the tradition of having her parents lift her veil and kiss her. She takes three steps away from them toward her new life.

Circling is an Orthodox custom in which the bride circles the groom three to seven times, symbolizing the entwining of their lives.

The *Kiddush* is the custom of passing wine to the groom and then to the bride as a sign of their commitment to their marriage.

The bride and groom are pronounced husband and wife in the *sheva b'rachot,* the Seven Blessings.

To a non-Jew, the most recognizable part of the Jewish wedding is the breaking of the glass. This has been said to represent many things, such as the destruction of the Temple in Jerusalem, the fragility of human relationships, or a reminder that sorrow dwells in the midst of joy. The guests all shout "*Mazel Tov*!" which is an expression of congratulations.

The bride and groom go into seclusion for ten or fifteen minutes. During this *yichud,* they have something to eat, since they have been fasting since morning.

The Buddhist Wedding Ceremony

Depending on the sect, the wedding ceremony can be held in a temple or at a special altar that has been set up elsewhere.

The ceremony begins with a chant by the priest, while everyone else meditates. This is followed by a typical ring ceremony. After the bride and groom place a pinch of incense at the altar before a statue of Buddha, they are pronounced husband and wife. They kiss. The priest delivers a short message and presents the couple with a new set of prayer beads or a book of Buddhist teachings.

The Islamic Ceremony

Before the wedding, the bride is presented with an agreed-upon *meher*, or mahr, which gives her security and freedom within the marriage. The *prompt* is the amount given to her upfront; the *deferred* will be given to her over the course of her husband's life. The groom proposes to his bride before two witnesses, who will also record the amount of the *meher*.

The wedding ceremony itself is similar to the typical Western ceremony, with a couple of exceptions. The marriage is a contract the couple has made with Allah, so the marriage can be officiated by any Muslim person. The sermon is likely to be in Arabic. There is no mention of the amount of the *meher* or the names of the witnesses.

African-American Weddings

Many North Americans of African descent incorporate the customs of their African ancestors into the traditional Christian wedding ceremony. One of the best known of these customs is "jumping the broom," which has its roots in the American South during the days of slavery. The broom's handle represents God, the many straws represent countless ancestors, and the binding of the broom symbolizes the couple's ties to their church, community, and family. The broom itself is a symbol of the couple's home. It can be decorated with flowers and ribbons to carry out the color scheme of the wedding.

The bride and groom can jump over the broom right after the benediction, as they enter the reception, before the first dance, or before they cut the wedding cake. If the broom jumping is to take place in the church, the best man or maid of honor will place it on the floor behind them. They will jump the broom, kiss, and proceed down the aisle.

Family members will often tie strips of cloth to the broom while they say a blessing for the marriage. To complete the ritual, couple ties a ribbon over these cloths. Miniature brooms make great favors for the guests.

The bride and groom often wear traditional African attire. Many decorate the wedding and reception with the colors of traditional Kente cloth–red, green, and black. Use it for napkins and tablecloths. Instead of throwing rice, guests can shower the newlyweds with kernels of corn.

Hispanic Weddings

Hispanic ceremonies are performed in English or Spanish, always in the Roman Catholic faith. An important part of the ceremony is the presentation of a Bible with the names of the bride and groom and their wedding date on the cover.

The *Arras* is a traditional part of the ceremony. Thirteen coins symbolize the twelve apostles and the bride and groom, who have now become one. The priest blesses the coins and hands them to the groom, who places them one by one in the bride's hand. The groom gives to share his wealth and the bride accepts to commit to using God's bounty to care for her family. The treasure box in which the coins are presented is often a family heirloom.

The *Lazo* or *Laso Rosary* is made of two loops of beads attached by a centerpiece and a crucifix. The bride and groom kneel with the Rosary around their shoulders, symbolizing their union in the Virgin Mary.

Instead of a veil, a Hispanic bride wears a *mantilla*, a lacy shawl-like head covering. She may carry a fan decorated with flowers instead of a bouquet. Although the traditional wedding dress resembles a Flamenco dancer's dress, the white wedding gown is now favored.

The mother of the bride is considered the most important in the Spanish wedding tradition, so she is escorted first. The women are escorted on the men's left side.

Padrios is the title given to a sponsor, who has a special place in the wedding ceremony. *Padrios* performs such tasks as presenting the Bible and placing the Rosary around the couple's shoulders. It is an honor to be asked to serve as *Padrios*.

The reception is a sit-down dinner, and the celebration lasts all night. Traditional foods include rice, chicken, beef, *paella*, tortilla dishes, and *tapa*. For the newlyweds' first dance, the guests gather to form a heart-shaped ring.

Chinese Weddings

Red and gold are the traditional Chinese wedding colors, symbolizing happiness and wealth, although many brides choose the white wedding gown and veil. The invitations can also be red, and don't overlook the possibilities for decorating the church and reception hall.

The traditional six ceremonies and five rituals have been modified, but some of the customs are still observed. Originally, the families of the bride and groom exchanged gifts that consisted of livestock, fowl, liquor, tea, jewelry, and wedding clothes. The marriage was confirmed by delivering the names of the bride's father, grandfather, and great-grandfather to the groom's family.

Traditionally, the bride's wedding-day bath was bamboo, pine, and artemisia for fortitude, longevity, prosperity, and purification. Friends of the groom arrived at the bride's home to escort her to him. Tea was shared with her family as a final farewell and to honor her ancestors. At the groom's home, the couple knelt together on a red mat or blanket for the marriage ceremony. The bride then served tea to her new in-laws, who presented her with gifts and money. Three days later, the bride would dress in her wedding clothes and be an invited guest in her family's home.

Today, a Ceremony of Obligation, honoring parents and elders, is a common part of Chinese wedding culture. Firecrackers and the Lion Dance are two favorite traditions, and gifts of money are usually given in red envelopes.

The tea which is served to parents and elders by the bride and groom contains lotus seeds and two red dates. This sweet tea is a wish for sweet relations between the two families. The newlyweds serve the tea in order, starting with the bride's mother, and use the formal titles "New Mother" and "New Father" to address their in-laws.

Candies with special meanings are distributed to the guests. Honey ginger candy ensures that the bride will speak only sweet words, but will also have some spicy qualities. Chocolate truffles are wrapped in the traditional red and gold. White rabbit candy represents a happy family, wealth, and children. Almond peanut candy asks for children and many blessings.

Japanese Shinto Weddings

Japanese weddings are usually held in the spring and fall. The Japanese calendar will determine the good days on which to be married and the bad days which are to be avoided.

Only the families attend the traditional wedding in the Shinto shrine. The bride dresses in a *kimono* with an *uchikake* (quilted robe) over it, and ties it with an *obi*. The groom wears a *kimono* and a *haori*, which is a kimono coat with the family crest on it.

Before the ceremony, the families enter and place upon the altar offerings of sake, rice water, salt, and fruit–everything to sustain life. The bride and groom are seated before the Shinto priest, with a mediator behind them. The families sit behind the mediator in order of age.

The ceremony lasts about fifteen minutes. The *Kannushi* (priest) waves a *tamagushi* branch over the couple to ward off evil spirits. The *Norito* (prayer/chant) announces the marriage to the gods. The bride and groom exchange a total of nine cups of sake, then the families share sake to symbolize their union through this marriage. They are assisted by serving girls called *miko*. Next, the bride and groom exchange rings. The groom reads a passage to pay homage to the gods, and the ceremony ends with the bride and groom saying their name.

There are no attendants. At the reception, the bride and groom sit at the head table with representatives from both families. Traditional food for the Japanese wedding is *tai* (the traditional fish of happiness), *sekihan* (red rice), *kombu* (kelp), and sake.

The traditional colors at the reception are red and white, the colors of the Japanese flag and a symbol of happiness. Another sign of celebration is the *kyogashi*, colorful candies made in the shapes of flowers.

Interfaith and Intercultural Weddings

An interfaith wedding is one in which the bride and groom are of different religions, although they may have lived next door to each other their whole lives, thereby sharing the same culture. An intercultural wedding is one in which the bride and groom are from different cultures. One may have grown up in North America and the other in the Philippines, although they share the same religion of Roman Catholicism.

The interfaith marriage is becoming more and more common. Naturally, both families want to see their faiths represented in the ceremony. Sit down with your families and decide what is important to each of them. Take notes, so that when you talk to the clergy you will have your priorities in front of you. Most of your ideas can be put into practice without offending either religion. The clergy will be most helpful in this regard.

Some religions are more accepting of interfaith marriages than others, and within each there are liberal and conservative lines. As a rule, there will be no problems with the Protestant denominations of Christianity, Shinto, Buddhist, Baha'i, and Hindu faiths. The Catholic Church is relaxing its rules, as is the Jewish faith. The Eastern Orthodox Church is open-minded, as long as the other partner is Christian. The Mormon Church will perform an interfaith ceremony, but not in a temple. In the Muslim faith, a woman can only marry a Muslim, but a man may also marry a Christian or Jewish woman.

Clergy from both religions will often perform a combined ceremony. Sacred writings of both can be read, such as the Bible, Torah, or Quran. If a combined ceremony is not possible, you can be married twice, once in your religion and once in that of your fiancé.

The reception will be a little easier. Set up food stations with both of your ethnic foods. Music of both cultures can be played, and perhaps flowers native to certain parts of the world can be incorporated into the flower arrangements. If one culture has different "wedding colors," they can form the color scheme.

Be sure the invitations reflect both cultures, whether in their design, their colors, or their language. Use a bilingual invitation if necessary. Print programs for the ceremony; this is the perfect place to introduce or explain a custom to guests who may be unfamiliar with it.

For Your Notes

CHAPTER 15

Double Weddings

Double weddings are rather uncommon. These weddings have their own special set of rules, but they can be handled quite easily if you keep your details straight. Double weddings take place when the brides are sisters or very close friends. Only rarely do we see a double wedding in which the grooms are brothers.

Invitations

If the brides are sisters, the invitations are issued by the parents. The elder sister is named first.

If the brides are not sisters, the two sets of parents can issue a joint invitation, or each family can issue their own invitation following the standard wording covered in Chapter 5. If the grooms are brothers, each bride's family issues a separate invitation.

The reception card for two sisters will follow the standard wording covered in Chapter 5.

Examples of invitation wording for two sisters, a joint invitation for brides who are not sisters, and a reception invitation follow on the next pages.

Examples of Invitation Wording

Example 1

Standard wording of a double wedding invitation, when the brides are sisters

Mr. and Mrs. George Alexander Aldridge
request the honour of your presence
at the marriage of their daughters
Laura Michelle
to
Mr. William David Taunton
and
Victoria Elizabeth
to
Mr. Patrick John Simpson
on Saturday, the tenth of June
two thousand and (year)
at one o'clock in the afternoon
Saint George's Anglican Church
Toronto, Ontario

Example 2

Standard wording of a double wedding invitation, when the brides are not sisters but wish to issue to a joint invitation

Mr. and Mrs. George Alexander Aldridge and
Mr. and Mrs. John Andrew Johnson
request the honour of your presence
at the marriage of their daughters
Laura Michelle Aldridge
to
Mr. William David Taunton
and
Mary Anne Johnson
to
Mr. David Michael Taylor
on Saturday, the tenth of June
two thousand and (year)
at one o'clock in the afternoon
Saint George's Anglican Church
Toronto, Ontario

Example of a Reception Invitation

Standard wording for the reception invitation of a double wedding, when the brides are not sisters

Mr. and Mrs. George Alexander Aldridge
and
Mr. and Mrs. John Andrew Johnson
request the pleasure of your company
on Saturday, the tenth of June
at seven o'clock in the evening
Beaumark Golf and Country Club
Toronto, Ontario

Seating the Parents

In a single-aisle church, if the brides are not sisters, both mothers are seated in the first pew, leaving room for their husbands. The mother of the older bride will be the last to be seated, and will sit by the aisle. If the mother of the younger bride prefers, she can be seated in the second pew, to be joined by her husband.

In a two-aisle church, if the brides are not sisters, each bride will have her own aisle. The older bride (Bride A) usually takes the left side. The parents of the bride and groom will sit on their respective sides of this aisle. Note that the parents of Groom A and the parents of Bride B are seated at opposite ends of the first pew in the center section. If the brides are sisters, use only one aisle.

For a Jewish wedding you don't have to worry about seating the parents. Your only concern is that the chuppah must be large enough to accommodate both weddings, with the parents at the chuppah's edge.

The Processional

If the church has two aisles, each wedding party can enter separately. If the brides are sisters, the brides' mother misses one processional to watch the other, so use only one aisle.

If there is only one aisle, there are different ways to handle the processional. On the next pages you will see two alternatives. In the first, the brides are sisters and are both escorted by their father. This may not be possible if the church has a narrow aisle. Note that in this example the ushers and bridesmaids are paired to allow for a shorter processional. The maids of honor remain separate.

In the second example, there is no pairing of the ushers and bridesmaids, and each bride is escorted by her father. If the brides are sisters, Bride A will be escorted by her father and Bride B by a close relative.

As you can see, this results in a very long processional. Both couples can share attendants if they wish. Even with separate wedding parties, they may choose to share a flower girl and ring bearer.

In both cases the grooms follow the clergy to the altar, accompanied by their best men.

Processional 1

Groom A / Best Man A / Clergy / Groom B / Best Man B
Usher A / Usher B
Usher A / Usher B
Usher A / Usher B
Bridesmaid A / Bridesmaid B
Bridesmaid A / Bridesmaid B
Bridesmaid A / Bridesmaid B
Maid of Honor A
Maid of Honor B
Flower Girl / Ring Bearer
Bride A / Father / Bride B

Processional 2

Groom A / Best Man A / Clergy / Groom B / Best Man B
Usher A
Usher A
Usher A
Usher B
Usher B
Usher B
Bridesmaid A
Bridesmaid A
Bridesmaid A
Maid of Honor A
Flower Girl A / Ring Bearer
A Bride A / Father
Bridesmaid B
Bridesmaid B
Bridesmaid B
Maid of Honor B
Flower Girl B/ Ring Bearer B
Bride B / Father or Relative

The Ceremony

If the brides are sisters, their father stands behind the older bride. The escort of the younger bride takes his seat. If the brides are not sisters, both fathers stand behind their daughters.

The older bride is given away first, then the younger, and the father(s) are seated.

The clergy will read the service to both couples. The sections requiring responses will be read first to the older bride and her groom, then to the younger.

Each bride can act as the other's maid of honor, holding her bouquet at the appropriate time in the ceremony. Likewise, each groom can act as the other's best man; however, he should hold his own bride's ring.

The Recessional

The recessional begins with the older bride and her groom, followed by the younger bride and her groom, both maids of honor with best men, the wedding party of the older bride, and the wedding party of the younger bride.

If the brides are not sisters, the parents of the older bride leave first, followed by the parents of the younger bride, then the parents of both grooms.

If both couples share attendants, there will be only one set of bridesmaids and one set of ushers. This means that there will be fewer people at the altar and less confusion during the processional and recessional. Highly recommended!

The flower girls and ring bearers will not take part in the recessional. On the next page, you will find the lineup for the recessional.

Example of a Recessional

Bridesmaid B / Usher B
Bridesmaid B / Usher B
Bridesmaid B / Usher B
Bridesmaid A / Usher A
Bridesmaid A / Usher A
Bridesmaid A / Usher A
Maid of Honor B / Best Man B
Maid of Honor A / Best Man A
Bride B / Groom B
Bride A / Groom A

The Receiving Line

If the brides are sisters, follow the receiving line etiquette from Chapter 13, placing the parents of the second groom beside those of the first. If the brides are not sisters, two lines are formed. However, if many of the guests are friends of both couples, one line will save time. The positions of each person will be as follows:

Mother of Bride A
Father of Bride A
Mother of Bride B
Father of Bride B
Mother of Groom A
Father of Groom A
Mother of Groom B
Father of Groom B
Maid of Honor A
Bride A
Groom A
Best Man A
Bridesmaids A alternating with Ushers A
Maid of Honor B
Bride B
Groom B
Best Man B
Bridesmaids B alternating with Ushers B

If the couples have acted as each other's maid of honor and best man, one line is required. In this case, each person will be positioned as follows:

Mother of Bride A
Father of Bride A
Mother of Bride B
Father of Bride B
Mother of Groom A
Father of Groom A
Mother of Groom B
Father of Groom B
Bride A
Groom A
Bride B
Groom B
Bridesmaids A alternating with Ushers A
Bridesmaids B alternating with Ushers B

In order to create a shorter receiving line, you may remove the grooms' fathers and the ushers. In this case, they will mingle with the guests.

The Reception

If the two couples served as each other's maid of honor and best man, there will be only one head table at the reception. Otherwise, there will be two separate tables.

The order of the first dances remains similar to that described in Chapter 13, with the following exceptions:

- Bride A and Groom A dance the first dance
- Bride B and Groom B dance the second dance
- Both brides dance with their fathers for the third dance. If the brides are sisters, they may each dance with their father for half the dance, the older bride first. Otherwise, they may have two father/daughter dances, or the younger bride can dance with an honored relative while her older sister dances with their father.
- Both grooms dance with their mothers for the fourth dance
- Bride A will throw her bouquet first, followed by Bride B.
- Groom A will throw the garter first, followed by Groom B.
- Both couples have their own wedding cake. Bride A and Groom A will cut theirs first, followed by Bride B and Groom B.

For Your Notes

CHAPTER

16

Theme Weddings

There are two types of theme weddings. The first is a well-researched reenactment of a wedding from a particular historical period or geographic area. There are wedding planners and set decorators who specialize in these types of weddings, so you will have no shortage of expert help in putting one together.

The second type of theme wedding is one in which you capture the ambiance and flavor without all of the details. These weddings are not restricted by the confines of particular theme, but are enhanced by them.

Some theme weddings involve guest participation, such as special dances or costumes, although many guests may feel uncomfortable and prefer to observe. If you are thinking of a theme wedding, keep in mind that they can cost considerably more than conventional weddings. Costumes must be rented; if the entire wedding party orders them at once, you may get a discount.

If the wedding will be in a church, costumes may not be allowed.

Hawaiian Theme

To create a Hawaiian atmosphere for your wedding, remember that a little goes a long way.

For flowers, start with orchids. Combined with ti leaves, they will give you a truly Hawaiian atmosphere. Orchids float, and can decorate a pool or fountain. Dendrobium orchids are non-toxic, so they can be floated in punch bowls. The Hawaiians believe that they bring good luck so they're perfect for a wedding!

Have the bridesmaids wear leis instead of carrying flowers. Give each female guest a flower to put behind her ear.

Be sure Hawaiian foods are on the menu. Some couples go so far as to plan a luau! Since ti leaves are non-toxic, they can be used to line the dishes. Have the wedding cake made without too much icing decoration, so that it can be decorated with dendrobium orchids.

Use pineapples, Hawaiian greenery, and coconut-scented candles as centerpieces. Have Hawaiian music playing quietly during the dinner. For an outdoor wedding, use tiki torches.

The invitations, favors (how about shark-tooth necklaces?) and even the gifts you give to your attendants can all fit easily into the Hawaiian theme.

Valentines Day Theme

A wedding that takes place on Valentine's Day would be a natural for this theme; think red, white, and pink. Be careful not to have too many hearts and cupids, and avoid cheap paper decorations. Decorate with plenty of tulle, topiaries with twinkling lights, and ribbons.

Red roses are a symbol of everlasting love, white roses represent purity, and pink roses are for passion.

Favors for the wedding guests are easy with this theme: it's safe to assume that anything heart-shaped or chocolate will be a hit, for example Hershey's Kisses in a heart-shaped trinket box.

Roaring Twenties Theme

Think of the 1920s and you think of gangsters, flappers, and the glamour of Hollywood; no wonder it's a favorite for theme weddings!

Your wedding dress can be a vintage gown of the era, perhaps even a family heirloom. Skirts were often pleated, and stockings had seams in the back. Have your bridesmaids dressed in fringed flapper dresses.

When decorating, use plenty of black, white, and silver.

The music you choose for dancing can include swing music and the Charleston. Have your groom learn it with you, so you can dazzle your guests! Jazz music played softly during dinner will also convey the mood of the 1920s.

There are many other ways to add the flavor of the era to this wedding, depending on how far you want to take it. Some couples recreate the speakeasy, complete with passwords at the door.

Beach Theme

Remember the Gidget movies of the 1950s? Or how about Frankie Avalon and Annette Funicello? No wonder beach-themed weddings are so popular!

To host a beach wedding, a private beach will allow you more control. A public beach will often be busy, especially on a beautiful summer night.

Decorate with seashells, tiki torches, sandcastles, surfboards, and tropical flowers. For the invitation, how about a message in a bottle?

Your dress can still be long and white, although a wedding gown is out of place here. A wreath of flowers in your hair is a nice alternative to the traditional veil. Some beach brides choose to be married in a bathing suit with a long wrap skirt, white of course.

Music can include Caribbean music, such as calypso. Don't forget the "summer songs" of the Beach Boys.

The menu should consist of foods you would typically find at beach parties: corn on the cob, a clam bake, or even a barbecue.

Favors can be anything related to sand and the sea. Consider small sandcastle replicas or fancy jars filled with shells.

Victorian Theme

The Victorian wedding theme is one of the most romantic because Queen Victoria and Prince Albert so obviously married for love. Before the age of movie stars, royalty was the main trendsetter, and Queen Victoria did not disappoint her subjects. The most important thing to remember when designing a Victorian wedding is that the emphasis is placed on beauty.

Victorian gowns have been reproduced in ivory tones to simulate aging, or you may be lucky enough to find a vintage gown. They are distinguished by a fitted bodice, gored skirt, and high-necked collar. They look good with a picture hat, flowers in the hair, or a floral wreath with an attached veil, as Queen Victoria wore. A cameo or brooch on the collar and perhaps a fan will accessorize in the Victorian fashion. Lockets and drop earrings were popular in the era. For a winter wedding, try a fur-trimmed cape and muff.

The bridesmaids' gowns will be similar to yours, but will differ in color and fabric.

Victorian grooms wore white tie and tails or a frock coat. Your groom can get the same effect with a rented morning coat. A top hat, walking stick, spats, and gloves will complete the look.

Until the Civil War, weddings were held at home. Victorian mansions can often be rented for weddings, receptions, and other occasions. The ceremony was held in the morning or late afternoon. Victorians held their receptions outdoors, but wedding ceremonies were always performed indoors. Perhaps you and your groom can arrive by horse and buggy.

Since Victorian weddings were often held in the morning, the reception following was called the "Wedding Breakfast." It could be served as a sit-down meal or a buffet, and was nothing at all like a breakfast! The wedding cake was the centerpiece of the wedding breakfast. Queen Victoria had a cake that weighed three hundred pounds! Traditional English fruitcake will provide the authentic touch. Champagne was used for toasting then as it is now. Cocktails such as mint juleps were popular, and Victorians were curious about a brand-new drink from America-Coca-Cola!

A charming Victorian custom was to have engagement and wedding rings of gemstones, each with a special meaning. The groom's birthstone was often the main stone in the bride's ring. Gemstones were used to spell words. For example, the first letters of ruby, emerald, garnet, amethyst, ruby, and diamond spell "regard."

Brides often spelled out the groom's name by using the first letter of each flower. This may result in a bouquet that will look a little different, but very Victorian. The most common bouquet style for the Victorian bride was the "tussy-mussy." The tussy-mussy is a small horn-shaped flower holder with a turn at the bottom for the bride to place over her finger. A single flower was placed into the horn and surrounded by a circle of smaller flowers, which were in turn surrounded by greenery.

Victorian wedding invitations were handmade of pressed flowers, lace, and ribbon.

Medieval or Renaissance Theme

The central theme for any medieval or Renaissance wedding is "amorem nostrum in aeterno," which is Latin for "our love is eternal."

Many churches and reception halls are built in the gothic style, making them the perfect backdrop for such a wedding. Decorate with wrought iron floor candelabra, banners, baskets of flowers, and lots of ivy. In order to get the atmosphere they want, some couples get married at a Renaissance Fair.

Wedding dresses of the period were dark green, burgundy, royal blue, or purple. Fabrics were frequently embellished with gold or silver metallic threads. Skirts were pleated, and bodices laced up the back. Long sleeves had leg-o-mutton styling. A band of blue was often used, since blue was the symbol of purity in the Middle Ages. This is where "something blue" came from. A Renaissance bride put on her right shoe first for luck, and she often tucked a silver coin into her left shoe to bring prosperity.

Guests who wish to indulge in the theme can simply add a cape and gloves to their usual formal wear.

Invitations are best done in calligraphy on ivory or beige parchment. They can be rolled like a scroll and perhaps sealed with wax.

Intersperse herbs such as rosemary, thyme, and basil among the flowers. To be very authentic, try to incorporate wheat into the bouquet. The bride's bouquet should be very large, and all bouquets should be hand-tied.

Handfasting was a medieval wedding ritual. During the wedding ceremony, the bride and groom faced each other. They placed their right hands and then their left hands together to form an infinity symbol while a cord was tied around their hands in a knot. In another version, the bride and groom placed their right hands together while a cord was used to tie a knot around their wrists.

Authentic foods from a medieval wedding feast include roast quail, partridge, goose, venison, cheese, walnuts, mulled wine, fruits, and ale-flavored bread.

Medieval guests brought small cakes to the wedding. These were piled onto one another and the bride and the groom had to kiss over them without toppling them. You may want to replace the traditional wedding cake with this ritual.

Disney Princess Theme

Little girls often dream of being a Disney Princess and having the fairy-tale wedding that goes with the dream. When they grow up, many brides make the fairy tale come true.

Some brides are married at Disney World, with Cinderella's pumpkin coach and all the trimmings, but just about every geographic area has a suitable location for such a wedding. Look for a historical building with a ballroom and access to a garden. Perhaps a mansion with a beautiful staircase will work well for you.

Decorate the venue with pastel colored tulle, satin ribbons, bows, birds, castles, roses, glitter, and maybe even a red carpet upon which you and your prince can make your grand entrance. Drape gossamer and netting around columns. To enhance the garden area, add trellises and arches, a decorated gazebo, and white chairs draped in tulle.

Have the invitations done in calligraphy. A scroll would be a nice touch, and can be mailed in special mailing tubes available at any office-supply store. Use red sealing wax to seal the invitations.

For your wedding colors, choose between pastels or jewel tones. Lavender, blue, pink, yellow, and ivory are all soft and delicate. Sapphire blues, amethysts, topaz, emerald greens, or ruby reds are all very regal.

You can wear a replica of a Disney gown, or a traditional white wedding gown. A tiara is a must! If Cinderella is your favorite princess, find a pair of Lucite shoes. You may even have your groom present you with one of them before you have your first dance, to the delight of your guests! Have your bridesmaids dressed in rich fabric, such as velvets or brocades.

As the bride (and a princess) you will probably carry roses. Red roses are the most elegant, but let your color scheme dictate. The bridesmaids can also carry bouquets of roses.

An ice sculpture would add the perfect touch to your reception. As for the favors, here's where you can have a bit of fun! Use small castles, glass slippers, or even little figurines of the Disney Princesses.

The music can come from the same enchanting films as the princesses themselves. For your first dance, waltz to "When You Wish Upon a Star," "A Whole New World," or "Someday My Prince Will Come."

As for transportation, a horse-drawn carriage is the perfect touch!

Western Theme

Want to "get hitched" in a country-western theme wedding?

Clothing for a western wedding is simple. You probably already have appropriate items in your closet already! The groom and his attendants can wear cowboy hats.

If you are located in the country, a barn will be the perfect setting for the reception. The western theme works best in an outdoor setting. Tablecloths can be made of red bandana fabric; hay and farm implements make perfect decorations.

Line dancing is a must at the reception! Have the DJ play country-western music, or if your budget allows, hire a country band.

You might want to leave with your groom on horseback, or by horse and buggy.

Be sure your neighbors know when the wedding will be held. Weddings and freshly fertilized fields don't mix!

A Christmas Wedding

A wedding held during the Christmas season allows you to take advantage of holiday decorations. For color schemes, you have three choices–the traditional red and green, white and silver, or white plus another color.

For a Christmas wedding, have your wedding gown trimmed in faux fur or wear a fur-trimmed cape over your gown. The bridesmaids can be dressed in velvet, perhaps burgundy or dark green.

A candlelit wedding ceremony is always especially meaningful at this time of year. Candles will be the main source of your Christmas wedding decorating, both in the church and in the reception hall. Many churches are decorated with poinsettias at this time of year, allowing you to save on flowers. Red roses are a perfect choice for your bouquet.

For your processional music, consider *Praise, My Soul, the King of Heaven.* The melody to this hymn is sung at Christmas time as the carol *Angels from the Realms of Glory.*

Decorations for a Christmas wedding consist of such things as glass or acrylic snowflakes, icicles, or Christmas ornaments. These can be clear, frosted, iridescent, or metallic. Centerpieces of evergreen, metallic ribbon in Christmas colors, and ball ornaments can adorn the tables.

Serve eggnog as well as punch before the reception. For the dinner itself, you may even decide on turkey and stuffing with cranberries.

Guests who bring gifts to the wedding can put them under a Christmas tree, which is decorated in your wedding colors.

Don't forget the mistletoe!

For Your Notes

CHAPTER 17

Destination Weddings

Simply put, a destination wedding is a wedding held in far-off place, often the honeymoon location. There are fewer guests, due to the travel involved.

Unless you are familiar with the venues and services of a specific location, you are best to hire a wedding planner. They fall into two categories: those who work with local clients to plan a wedding at the destination point, and those who are located at the destination point and work long-distance with their clients.

If you use a wedding planner, hire one who has training in travel and tourism. Some can book airline tickets and hotels, but you may prefer to book through a regular travel agent.

Will Guests be Invited?

Some couples bring along a few guests, even just two special people to stand up for them. Others prefer to travel alone, and have their marriage witnessed by court employees.

Two things will determine if you will be inviting guests–location and finances.

If the destination is a remote, romantic spot, you will probably want to be alone. On the other hand, a busy tourist resort will have plenty for the guests to do. After the wedding, you go on your honeymoon, and they go on vacation.

The only expenses you are expected to incur are the hotel accommodations for your wedding party. They pay for their own airfare and meals. Guests pay for their own airfare, accommodations and meals.

Because of the added expense, many of your guests will have to decline the invitation. In this case, you may wish to have a reception when you return home, complete with a video of your wedding. Don't be hurt if friends or family are unable to attend; the costs can be prohibitive. Send invitations to everyone you want to include, even if you know their financial situation. That way, they won't feel snubbed. It's their option to decline.

If the wedding is to include guests and will be held at a location where admission is charged, enclose an admission card with their invitation. See Chapter 5 for more information on admission cards. If your guests are staying at a different resort, they may incur a "day fee" to attend your wedding. Strictly speaking, you should pay for that as well.

European Weddings

Perhaps you want to get married in a place to which you once travelled, or one that you have always wanted to see. Maybe you have a special attachment to a particular movie and wish to be married "on location" where it was filmed. Paris, London, and Rome are favorites. So are the less populous areas, such as Tuscany and the Greek Islands.

If you like to ski, the Swiss or Austrian Alps offer the perfect wedding/honeymoon location.

In Europe, clergy does not act on behalf of the state. Therefore, they require that a religious ceremony be preceded by a civil ceremony. Strapless wedding gowns, and those with low necklines, are not always acceptable. Each country has different residency requirements and your documents must be translated into the local language. To investigate the requirements for the country in which you wish to be married, contact their consulate office. The legal requirements for several countries appear at the end of this chapter.

Hawaiian and Las Vegas Weddings

These are both popular with residents of the other states. You can have a wedding away, while still in your own country.

Hawaii is a favorite, as it offers such a variety of picturesque locations. Couples marrying in Hawaii can choose from many beautiful parks, or they can marry at Iolani Palace, the site of royal weddings. Pagoda Waterfall, Maui, and Waikiki Beach are also in demand. The most beautiful of all Hawaiian customs is the exchange of leis by the bride and groom.

The State of Hawaii requires a marriage license, purchased in advance of the wedding date. There are no health requirements or blood tests, but both the bride and the groom must be present. Nonresidents of the United States must provide passports. Check with local officials for the waiting period.

Weddings are big business in Las Vegas. Couples stand in line for up to five hours to be married on Valentine's Day. The city is home to countless wedding chapels and even drive-through chapels.

Wedding themes are right at home in Las Vegas. You can have anything from Star Wars to Elvis (he and Priscilla were married here in 1967.) Some chapels offer ceremonies in different languages.

Although Las Vegas has a reputation for "quickie" marriages, there are still legalities to be considered. The State of Nevada requires a valid marriage license; their County Courthouse is open twenty-four hours on holidays! There are no blood tests or waiting periods.

Cruises

Cruises have long been a favorite honeymoon option; lately, they have become popular for weddings, too! Cruises can be booked on ships that hold fewer than one hundred people or over two thousand. They travel to almost any destination that can be reached by water.

Budgeting is simple–everything is included, with the exception of drinks, onshore excursions, personal services, and tips. Depending upon the ports-of-call, a passport will be necessary.

As for the actual wedding, shop around for the cruise line first, and then inquire. Special programs are available which allow couples to be married in port. They will be governed by the regulations of that particular location.

The Disney Wedding

Disney World in Orlando, Florida, offers complete wedding packages for the young-at-heart. As a company renowned for its attention to detail, Disney holds nothing back in achieving perfection. Wedding ceremonies are held in the Disney Wedding Pavilion, with receptions at one of three Disney resorts.

Your first stop will be your real-life fairy godmother: Disney's wedding planner. Together, you will begin to spin your plans into reality.

Music for the wedding reception can be a single harp, a big band, or anything in between. The menu will be prepared by some of the world's finest chefs. Everything from flowers to photography is expertly planned and executed.

Epcot offers the opportunity to have a wedding with an international flavor. Or, you can be Cinderella, complete with a glass coach and an after hours reception in the Magic Kingdom's castle. Whatever your choice, you and your prince will cut your wedding cake under fireworks. Even the Disney characters will be there to share your happiness!

Traveling with Your Wedding Gown

If you will be taking the gown on a cruise ship or traveling by car, add a little extra tissue and hang it in your cabin or lay it across the back seat.

If you will be traveling by plane, ask the bridal boutique to pack it for you. If they don't have a box large enough (and this is often the case) use a suitcase.

To pack the gown yourself, line the suitcase with plenty of tissue. Place the center of the gown on the suitcase, face down. Fold the skirt lengthwise to fit the suitcase; use tissue for padding. Fold the bottom of the skirt into the suitcase, again using lots of tissue, and then the bodice. If the dress moves around when you move the suitcase, open it and add more tissue.

As soon as you reach your destination, unpack the gown and hang it in the bathroom. Close the door and turn on the shower. Be sure the gown will not get splashed; you merely want the steam from the shower to take care of the wrinkles. A hand steamer may be needed for stubborn creases.

If you are traveling to an area where a professional dry cleaning service is available through your hotel, have them freshen your gown for you.

Other Considerations

Budget: Destination weddings have many unique expenses, but the advantage is that the honeymoon is already taken care of. Consider travel costs, plus the usual: attire, photographer, and flowers.

Documentation: Each destination has its own requirements. Providing the necessary documents is the responsibility of the bride and groom. You must find out which are needed (birth certificate, passport, proof of divorce) as well as whether the documents must be originals (or if a copy or a certified copy is permissible.) Some countries require that the documents be translated.

Filing and waiting period: In some countries, documentation must be sent on ahead. How far in advance? After the license has been issued, how long must you wait to get married? Can you get the license in advance or must you wait until your arrival?

Residency requirements: Some countries have none. Others require that you live in the district for certain length of time.

Ceremony: Can the ceremony be performed in English? If not, will a translator be provided?

Medical: Are blood tests or medical exams necessary? If so, are they to be performed at home or at the destination? Are inoculations required?

Witnesses: Are they needed? How many? Some countries require that the witnesses be residents. In this case, they can usually be provided for you.

Legal Requirements by Location

Canada: Marriage license applications are filed with the clerk from any municipal office. It is necessary to show a birth certificate and proof of divorce. The fee varies from province to province.

United States: Marriage license applications are filed with the clerk from any municipal office. It is necessary to show a birth certificate and in some states, a social security number. You must also show proof of divorce. The fee varies from state to state.

Europe: Church weddings are performed only after a civil ceremony. Marriage license applications are filed with the clerk from any municipal office. It is necessary to show a birth certificate and proof of divorce. In some countries, this is in the form of an affidavit stating that you are legally allowed to marry. The fee varies, depending upon the country. In some countries there may be a residency requirement. Many countries require medical certificates, translated into their own language or issued by their own doctors.

France: French law dictates that banns must be published. Two months before this, you must provide a medical certificate with the results of blood tests. It is preferable that the test be done in France, but a doctor outside France can perform the test, as long as the French consulate approves him. The residency period is forty days (thirty for the license plus ten for the publication of the banns). If either of you has been married before, you must provide a *certificate de coutme*, verifying that you are free to marry in France and that the marriage will be valid in your own country. You also need an affidavit explaining the termination of previous marriages, and birth certificates. An approved lawyer must translate all documents into French.

Italy: You must provide divorce or death certificates, as well as *Atto Notorio*, which is a declaration that there is nothing in your country's laws to prevent you from being married. If you are under eighteen, you need sworn consent from your parents. A woman whose previous marriage was terminated within the last three hundred days must obtain a waiver from the *Procura* *della Republica* (District Attorney), which is issued on presentation of a medical certificate that she is not pregnant. You can marry in either a civil or religious ceremony in Italy. There are limited residency requirements. A local civil official must perform the marriage. The marriage cannot be performed on the premises of a foreign embassy or consulate. If a Roman Catholic priest is performing the marriage, you do not need to get married first in a civil ceremony; however, the priest must register the marriage with the civil registrar in order for the marriage to be legal. If you are non-Roman Catholic, a prior civil ceremony is usually required to ensure the legality of the marriage. Civil ceremonies must take place in a Town Hall or property purchased by the local government. Palaces, villas and manors are settings that are approved for civil ceremonies.

Bahamas: Apply in person to a Bahamas notary public or your own embassy in Nassau. You must have obtained proof of single status from your consulate before leaving home. Birth certificates, passports, and photo ID are required. There is waiting period of one day after the license is issued. There is no residency requirement.

Jamaica: Apply for a marriage license at the Ministry of National Security in Kingston. Residency of twenty-four hours is required and there is a one-day waiting period after the license is issued. If you are under twenty-one, you must provide proof of parental consent. Photo ID and proof of citizenship, a birth certificate with your father's name, and death or divorce certificates are required for second marriages.

Mexico: Apply at the *Registro Civil* in the city in which you wish to be married. You need your passport, birth certificate, tourist cards, and Visa. As well, you must provide the names, addresses, ages, and tourist cards of four witnesses. A blood test is required, which must be performed in Mexico. There is a two-day residency requirement (except Cozumel) and there is a waiting period of two to four days.

British Virgin Islands: Apply in person at the Attorney General's office in Tortola on the day of arrival. You need a passport, birth certificate, and proof of death or divorce. There is no residency requirement, but there is a three-day waiting period.

Dominican Republic: You must send a written request for permission to marry to your embassy in Santo Domingo. Witnesses must be non-family. Passports for you and your witnesses, as well as originals of birth certificates and divorce/death certificates are required. First/middle/last names must be identical on all pieces of ID. The Dominican consulate or your embassy must translate documents into Spanish. There is no residency requirement.

For Your Notes

CHAPTER 18

Home Weddings

Home weddings invoke a sentimental ambiance that no other wedding can. Imagine this:

- a bride gliding gracefully down the staircase on her father's arm, the same staircase she once slid down–very *un*gracefully
- a bride in her grandmother's backyard, carrying a bouquet of freshly-picked wildflowers
- a bride and groom getting married in the home they will share for years to come

Locations for Home Weddings

Garden weddings are especially beautiful, and they are already decorated for you! The major drawback, of course, is the unpredictability of the weather. Plan for a tented reception. For an outdoor wedding ceremony, rent an arbor or use an especially beautiful area of the garden. If the weather turns bad, the tent can also accommodate the ceremony.

Indoors, home weddings are sheltered from the elements, but the average home lacks the space that other venues provide. Therefore, home weddings are much smaller. When planning the reception, examine the space available. Furniture will most likely need to be moved, and in extreme cases, removed to storage to make room for rented tables.

When you are planning the indoor space, don't overlook space for a rented bar (if the home does not already have one) and a dance floor. If you will be hiring a DJ, he will need space as well. As you can see, this is becoming quite an exercise in space planning; make scaled floor plans of each room.

Style and Formality

The style and formality of the wedding must be in keeping with the style and formality of the home. A formal wedding would be more appropriate in a formal home than in a log home in the country.

The color scheme of the wedding must not clash with the color scheme of the home. That is not to say that the colors should be identical. Contrasts can be beautiful.

Decorations for a home wedding will be much simpler. The floral arrangements should be fewer and smaller. In fact, flowers and candles are all the decoration you will need.

Outdoors, citronella will help to keep the bugs away. Use it in the candles or in hurricane lamps on the tables.

Guests and Invitations

The guest list for a home wedding will be limited to the number of people the home can comfortably hold. If a tent is used, the guest list can be larger. Regardless of its size, the guest list is divided between the bride, the groom, and their families, as discussed in Chapter 4.

The invitations are similar to those for a church wedding, with a couple of changes. Home weddings always use "the pleasure of your company" instead of "the honour of your presence." The home address appears in the invitation, but "at our home" does not. The invitations that follow show the standard wording for a home wedding. Note that the invitation is always issued by the person at whose home the wedding will be held.

Announcements are sent out by the person who hosted the wedding or by the bride and groom themselves. "At our home" replaces the address, or can be omitted altogether.

While we're on the subject of guests, give early consideration to parking. Avoid causing a neighborhood disruption by using a nearby school or shopping plaza, if possible.

Examples of Invitation Wording

Example 1

Example of a wedding invitation for a home wedding issued by the bride's parents

Mr. and Mrs. George Alexander Aldridge
request the pleasure of your company
at the marriage of their daughter
Laura Michelle
to
Mr. William David Taunton
on Saturday, the tenth of June
two thousand and (year)
at three o'clock in the afternoon
123 Garden Street
Toronto, Ontario

Example 2

Example of a wedding invitation for a home wedding issued by the groom's parents

Mr. and Mrs. James Edward Taunton
request the pleasure of your company
at the marriage of
Miss Laura Michelle Aldridge
to their son
Mr. William David Taunton
on Saturday, the tenth of June
two thousand and (year)
at three o'clock in the afternoon
123 Garden Street
Toronto, Ontario

Example 3

Example of a wedding invitation for a home wedding issued by the bride and groom

Laura Michelle Aldridge and
William David Taunton
request the pleasure of your company
at their marriage
on Saturday, the tenth of June
two thousand and (year)
at three o'clock in the afternoon
123 Garden Street
Toronto, Ontario

Examples of Announcements

Example 1

Standard wording of a wedding announcement issued by the parents

Mr. and Mrs. George Alexander Aldridge
have the honour of announcing
the marriage of their daughter
Laura Michelle
to
Mr. William David Taunton
on Saturday, the tenth of June
two thousand and (year)
(location not necessary)

Example 2

Standard wording of a wedding announcement issued by the couple

Miss Laura Michelle Aldridge
and
Mr. William David Taunton
announce their marriage
on Saturday, the tenth of June
two thousand and (year)

Example 3

Alternate wording of a wedding announcement, including the location

The marriage of
Miss Laura Michelle Aldridge
and
Mr. William David Taunton took place
on Saturday, the tenth of June
two thousand and (year)
at their home
in Toronto, Ontario

The Ceremony

Like a church ceremony, the home wedding ceremony will take place at the altar. Use a fireplace if one is available. Otherwise, the altar will be wherever you set up a floral decoration, a table for signing the register, and perhaps a pair of floor candelabra.

For a Jewish wedding, a chuppah will be erected.

Once the altar location has been determined, rented chairs can be set up, forming an "aisle" leading to the altar. If a large guest list makes chairs impractical, guests can stand on either side. Be sure to provide seating for those who need it.

The aisle can be defined by using an aisle runner, but this is not absolutely necessary indoors. Outdoors, a runner will prevent grass stains on the hems of skirts and will keep high heels from sinking into the ground. To make it sturdier, have plywood placed beneath it. Another word of warning: cut the grass a few days before. Freshly cut grass and weddings don't mix!

The processional and recessional music can be provided by an organ or piano, a soloist, a trio or quartet, or recorded music. For an outdoor ceremony, a portable keyboard may be the answer. The DJ who will be providing the reception music can also handle the ceremony. Be sure there are enough electrical outlets and extension cords.

After the ceremony you can form a receiving line if you wish. Otherwise, make a point of mingling and chatting with each guest.

The Reception

A wedding reception at home is entertaining on a grand scale. Often, a decision to have a home wedding is based on a misconception that it will save money, but what you save on the venue you will spend on rentals and other incidentals.

Many home receptions feature sit-down meals served buffet-style, which takes a great deal of space. Others take the form of a cocktail reception, where only finger food is served. The afternoon tea, featuring sandwiches, a cheese tray, and a vegetable/fruit platter is another option.

The types of wedding receptions discussed in Chapter 13 also apply to those held at home. In addition, you can have a "stand-up" reception, where guests nibble as they mingle. This differs from a cocktail reception in that the food is more substantial. You may even decide on a dessert reception, with the wedding cake as the highlight, of course!

Some couples do the cooking for the reception, with help from close family members. This is too much work for a large reception. Although a professional caterer is much more expensive, it is money well spent. Depending on the size of the family kitchen, food can be cooked on-site, or it can be cooked and transported to the home, where it will be kept warm until serving time. If the kitchen is just *too* small, the caterer can set up a complete kitchen in a tent.

The wedding cake is the centerpiece of the reception. Be sure it is placed in a cool area.

A scaled floor plan will help you set up the tables for the reception. Rented tables and chairs, china, silver, glassware, linens, and serving dishes come in a wide variety of styles and colors to match the ambiance of any wedding. Your rental company will be able to assist you in the selection of all these.

If there will be dancing, the DJ will set up near a rented dance floor. As a professional, he will be aware of the acoustical differences between a home and a reception hall, and will make the necessary adjustments. Remember to turn off the music after eleven o'clock!

Professional bartenders can be hired and a Special Occasion Permit or liquor license may be needed. Check your local laws.

Home receptions include all of the traditions–the speeches and toasts, the first dance, and the throwing of the bouquet. Much of the information in Chapter 13 applies here.

The Wedding Cake

Since a home wedding will most likely have fewer guests, the cake will be smaller. As with all weddings, it will be the focal point of the reception. Even if the reception does not include a sit-down meal, the wedding cake is a must. All cakes for home weddings should be tiered, even a cake for a very small gathering. Since there will be fewer tiers, and each will be smaller in diameter, it will look better if they are separated by pillars.

Although a selection of desserts will also be offered, the wedding cake is served as the last course. Hopefully, you have a friend or relative who is skilled at cake cutting. After the pictures have been taken, they will take the cake to the kitchen, cut it and place it onto plates to be served. As a lovely alternative, you and your groom can cut the cake right at the table, chatting with your guests as you do. Whoever will be cutting the wedding cake should practice on simple cakes until they get the knack.

Floor Plan

Use this page to sketch a floor plan of your home to help with the placement of guest tables and other elements of your home wedding.

For Your Notes

CHAPTER 19

Military Weddings

Invitations

Certain etiquette applies to the wording and addressing of wedding invitations. The groom's rank may be included in his name, as in "Major James Robert Wilson." His designation will appear on the next line, as in "United States Army." For a lower rank, the name and designation appear as above, but without the rank. "Mr." is omitted. No abbreviations of rank or title are permitted. Check with the authorities for the country in which you live. Here are the general rules:

- Army: Captain and above, use rank with name, as in "Major James Robert Wilson"
- Army: Sergeant to Captain, use rank with designation, as in "Sergeant, United States Army"
- Army: Below Sergeant, use designation only, as in "United States Army"
- Air Force: Sergeant and above, use rank with name
- Force: Below Sergeant, use designation only
- Navy: Commander and above, use rank with name
- Navy: Below Commander, use rank and designation only
- Navy: No rank, use designation only
- Marine Corps: Major and above, use rank with name
- Marine Corps: Below Major, use rank with designation
- Marine Corps: Below Sergeant, use designation only

Retired high-ranking officers are treated as above. The word "Retired" will appear after the designation on the same line, separated by a comma.

If the bride is in the service, she will use the above form if she and the groom are issuing the invitations. If the bride's parents are issuing the invitations, the standard form is used, without her rank and designation.

The outer envelope of the invitation will include the addressee's name and rank, followed by the address. The designation is not used. For example, "Major John Philip Sanderson," or "Major and Mrs. John Philip Sanderson." The inner envelope will read, "Major Sanderson," or "Major and Mrs. Sanderson."

Dress and the Wedding Party

Members of the military can wear their dress uniform or a tuxedo. If the bride is in the service, she may wear her dress uniform or a traditional wedding gown. The bride's attire determines the degree of formality for the rest of the wedding.

The wedding party can be military, civilian, or mixed. There will be as many ushers as there are bridesmaids, or as many as it takes to seat the guests. If some ushers are civilian and some are military, they are paired alike for the recessional, since civilians do not take part in the arch of swords or sabers.

With a regulation uniform, medal ribbons are worn. With a dress uniform, wear large medals, and with a dinner jacket, miniatures. Boutonnieres are never worn on a uniform.

Bridesmaids may wear traditional bridesmaid dresses. The bride and her attendants carry flowers, but corsages are never worn on a uniform.

The Ceremony

The military wedding ceremony is identical to the civilian until the recessional.

If the bride or her father are active members of the Armed Forces, the ceremony will be presided over by their chaplain. If the bride and her father are civilians, the ceremony will be performed by the clergy of the bride's choosing, perhaps the groom's chaplain.

Regimental flags may decorate the church; the usual floral arrangements are proper.

Seating is according to rank. Some officers are assigned special pews.

The Recessional and the Arch of Swords

The arch of sabers takes place at the altar. When the bride and groom stand after the benediction, the head usher gives the commands, "Center face" and "Arch sabers." The sabers are arched with points touching and cutting edge up. After the bride and groom pass through, he commands, "Carry sabers" and "Rear face." The ushers leave in pairs down the aisle, and the recessional proceeds as usual. The arch is formed again on the steps of the church, this time with swords.

In preparation for the arch of swords, the wedding party, parents, and chaplain leave the church. The bride and groom will go immediately to the anteroom. At this time, the ushers will direct the guests outside the church so that the arch can be formed.

Members of the wedding party line up on the steps on either side of the door. The ushers take their places facing each other in equal numbers, and the best man signals the bride and groom.

When the head usher commands, the ushers draw their swords in one continuous motion, tips touching. The bride and groom are the only ones to pass under the arch. When ordered to return their swords, they leave about three inches out of the scabbard, and then return home in a single click.

Cake Cutting and Toasts

The military reception is identical to the civilian reception, with two exceptions: cutting the wedding cake and the best man's toast.

The groom's sword or saber is used to cut the wedding cake instead of the customary silver knife. It goes without saying that it must never be decorated with ribbons or flowers. The groom places his right hand over the bride's right hand, as in any other wedding.

When the best man proposes the first toast, he welcomes the bride into the service. Make sure that his notes, and those of the Master of Ceremonies, recognize the ranks of all officers present.

Invitation Wording

Example 1

Standard invitation wording if the bride's father is in the military

Captain and Mrs. Marvin Paul Jones
request the honour of your presence
at the marriage of their daughter
Marie Joyce
to
Mr. Peter Roy Spencer
on Saturday, the tenth of June
two thousand and (year)
at three o'clock in the afternoon
Saint Mary's Episcopalian Church
New York, New York

Example 2

Standard invitation wording if the groom is in the military

Mr. and Mrs. Marvin Paul Jones
request the honour of your presence
at the marriage of their daughter
Marie Joyce
to
Peter Roy Spencer
Sergeant, United States Air Force
on Saturday, the tenth of June
two thousand and (year)
at three o'clock in the afternoon
Saint Mary's Episcopalian Church
New York, New York

Example 3

Standard invitation wording if the bride is in the military

Mr. and Mrs. Marvin Paul Jones
request the honour of your presence
at the marriage of their daughter
Marie Joyce Jones
to
Mr. Peter Roy Spencer
on Saturday, the tenth of June
two thousand and (year)
at three o'clock in the afternoon
Saint Mary's Episcopalian Church
New York, New York

For Your Notes

CHAPTER 20

Second Weddings

Much of the etiquette surrounding second marriages centers on the bride. If this is her first marriage and the groom's second, there are no restrictions. A first-time bride marrying a widowed or divorced groom may have the wedding of her dreams.

Although etiquette rules are starting to relax, a second wedding should never pretend to be a first. That does not mean that it will be any less formal, just that some of the traditional components will be changed.

Other than those details covered in this chapter, the wedding-planning process for a second wedding is similar to the planning of the first wedding.

What's Changed?

Forty years ago, a second-time bride wore a corsage on her suit and celebrated with her groom at their favorite restaurant. Today, flowers, gowns, dancing, and sit-down dinners are becoming the norm rather than the exception.

Many second-time brides now wear white. White is the color traditionally associated with purity, hence its popularity for wedding gowns. Today, white is associated with all brides.

The second-time bride can be escorted up the aisle by her father, but she is not given away. She might chose to walk alone, or be met halfway by the groom.

Gifts

Strictly speaking, a bride should receive wedding gifts only once. However, this is the most-broken rule in the etiquette books! Almost all guests, even if they attended your first wedding, will want to send a gift.

It is still considered in poor taste to register twice for gifts. Besides, wedding guests know that you have already set up your household or are perhaps merging two separate households. You don't want or need another toaster!

Gifts for couples marrying for the second time are quite different. You are more likely to be presented with your favorite wine, a pair of theatre tickets, or a cash gift.

Couples who have everything they need often hint to their friends that a donation to charity is the best gift of all.

All etiquette surrounding the recording and acknowledging of gifts goes unchanged. Refer to Chapter 4.

Former In-Laws and Children from Previous Marriages

If you have been widowed, your friendships with members of your late husband's family may have continued. You may certainly invite them to the wedding. You might even treasure your friendship with a former sister-in-law so much that you would like her to stand up for you. Be careful not to hurt anyone's feelings. Speak to your fiancé and make sure he doesn't object to your former in-laws attending. Chances are, he'll be fine with the idea. The same goes for the groom who wants to include his late wife's family. You must also realize that your former in-laws may have mixed feelings about your remarriage. Openly discuss the subject with everyone involved.

I admire those who are able to remain on friendly terms after a divorce, especially if there are young children involved. However, I would advise against inviting an ex-spouse to the wedding, on the grounds that it is sure to make the second spouse rather uncomfortable. Still, it would be a nice gesture to let your "ex" hear the news firsthand.

The children of the first marriage deserve special consideration, especially if they are feeling displaced. Whenever possible, include them in the wedding party, according to their ages.

Legalities

The most important legal aspect is the dissolution of the first marriage.

A widow or widower is free to marry again, even in the Catholic Church, one of the strictest on the subject.

A person who has been divorced cannot remarry in the Catholic Church unless the first marriage is annulled. Other religions and denominations are more relaxed on this matter, and may agree to a church wedding after interviewing the couple.

Whatever the situation, the second marriage will be subject to the same regulations as the first–the marriage license, waiting times, residency requirements, and medical or blood tests needed.

As well as documentation of age and citizenship, you must provide proof of divorce or annulment. If either of you was divorced outside the country you may need a lawyer's letter to accompany the documents. In some areas, a widow or widower may be asked for a death certificate.

Invitations

If the bride has been using her former married name, it will appear on the wedding invitations. Likewise, if she has gone back to her maiden name, that is the name that will be used on the invitations.

Most invitations to second weddings are issued by the couple themselves. However, parents sometimes host the wedding and issue the invitations when a very young bride has been divorced or widowed.

Examples follow on the next pages.

Examples of Invitations

Example 1

Standard wording for the invitation when the bride and groom host the second wedding in the church

The honour of your presence is requested
at the marriage of
Mary Jane Smith
to
Joseph Edward Winslow
Saturday, the tenth of June
two thousand and (year)
at three o'clock in the afternoon
Saint George's Anglican Church
Toronto, Ontario

Example 2

Alternative wording for the invitation when the bride and groom host the second wedding in the church

Mary Jane Smith
and
Joseph Edward Winslow
request the honour of your presence
at their marriage
Saturday, the tenth of June
two thousand and (year)
at three o'clock in the afternoon
Saint George's Anglican Church
Toronto, Ontario

Example 3

Standard wording for the invitation when the bride and groom host the second wedding at a location other than a church

The pleasure of your company is requested
at the marriage of
Mary Jane Smith
to
Joseph Edward Winslow
Saturday, the tenth of June
two thousand and (year)
at three o'clock in the afternoon
Fairview Country Club
Toronto, Ontario

Example 4

Alternative wording for the invitation when the bride and groom host the second wedding at a location other than a church

Mary Jane Smith
and
Joseph Edward Winslow
request the pleasure of your company
at their marriage
Saturday, the tenth of June
two thousand and (year)
at three o'clock in the afternoon
Fairview Country Club
Toronto, Ontario

Example 5

Standard wording for the invitation when the parents host the second wedding in the church

Mr. and Mrs. George Scott Miller
request the honour of your presence
at the marriage of their daughter
Mary Jane Smith
(her married surname)
to
Joseph Edward Winslow
Saturday, the tenth of June
two thousand and (year)
at three o'clock in the afternoon
Saint George's Anglican Church
Toronto, Ontario

Example 6

Standard wording for the invitation when the parents host the second wedding at a location other than a church

Mr. and Mrs. George Scott Miller
request the pleasure of your company
at the marriage of their daughter
Mary Jane Smith
to
Joseph Edward Winslow
Saturday, the tenth of June
two thousand and (year)
at three o'clock in the afternoon
Fairview Country Club
Toronto, Ontario

For Your Notes

CHAPTER 21

Renewing Your Wedding Vows

A ceremony in which a married couple renews their wedding vows is called a reaffirmation. In this age of divorce, it's a wonderful thing to see! The ceremony can take the form of a formal wedding, a semiformal affair in a rented banquet hall, an informal home buffet or cocktail party, or anything in between. Some have themes, like the couple who recreated their Hawaiian honeymoon!

There are many reasons to renew your wedding vows. Perhaps you eloped and never got to have the lavish wedding of your dreams. Maybe you've weathered many storms together; you may have even been separated for a while. Or, you may be celebrating a milestone, such as a twenty-fifth anniversary.

If this is to be a formal affirmation, you can choose bridesmaids, ushers, a maid of honor, and a best man. Perhaps you can ask the same friends who stood up for you at your first wedding.

There are similarities between weddings and vow renewals, but etiquette can be adapted and even invented in this case. As an added bonus, there are no legalities to worry about. Most couples have their original rings re-blessed or buy new eternity rings. Others consider this the perfect time for the huge diamond they couldn't afford all those years ago!

Invitations

Invitations can be formal, informal, or handwritten. It all depends on the formality of the ceremony and reception.

The styles, font, and colors in wedding stationery catalogues are also perfect; simply change the wording. You may wish to design and print your own invitations on your computer. Have extras for keepsakes.

Use a reply card for a formal affair. For informal invitations, a telephone number is often provided as a way for guests to RSVP.

Use a separate reception card for a formal reaffirmation. Otherwise, include the reception information on the invitation.

Examples of invitations follow on the next four pages.

Examples of Invitation

Example 1

Standard invitation wording for a vow renewal to take place in a church

John and Cynthia Adams
request the honour of your presence
at the reaffirmation of their wedding vows
on Saturday, the tenth of June
two thousand and (year)
at one o'clock in the afternoon
Saint George's Anglican Church
Toronto, Ontario

Example 2

Invitation wording for a vow renewal to take place at a location other than a church

On the occasion
of their twenty-fifth wedding anniversary
John and Cynthia Adams
request the pleasure of your company
as they renew their wedding vows
Saturday, the tenth of June
two thousand and (year)
at three o'clock in the afternoon
123 Garden Street
Toronto, Ontario

RSVP by August 1
Best wishes only

Example 3

A more informal wording for a vow renewal invitation

Please join us
as we renew our wedding vows
on Saturday, the tenth of June
two thousand and (year)
at three o'clock in the afternoon
123 Garden Street
Toronto, Ontario
and buffet following
John and Cynthia Adams

RSVP 555-1234
Best wishes only

Example 4

Wording for vow renewal invitations issued by the children of the couple

Tyler and Olivia
invite you to join friends and family
at the reaffirmation ceremony of our parents
John and Cynthia Adams
Saturday, the tenth of June
two thousand and (year)
at one-thirty in the afternoon
123 Garden Street
Toronto, Ontario
and afterwards at Shalimar Restaurant

555-1234
Best wishes only

Guests and Gifts

The general rule about the bride and groom dividing the guest list doesn't apply here. Although you will both have friends that you wish to invite, many will be mutual friends. Some may have been invited to your first wedding, and, of course, there are the friends you've met since!

Although it isn't appropriate for you to register for gifts, many people wouldn't dream of attending a wedding, even a renewal of vows, empty-handed. As with a second wedding, guests understand that you already have what you need for your home. They will give you such gifts as wine, theatre tickets, cash or gift certificates, or a donation to your favorite charity.

The words "Best wishes only" are often added to the invitation. You may also say, "The only presents we require is your presence with us."

Attire

The only rule regarding wedding attire is that you must be in keeping with the formality of the occasion.

Perhaps you would like to wear your original wedding gown or the gown you didn't get to wear the first time. Have alterations done ahead of time. If the dress can be zipped up, there is usually enough fabric in the seams to allow a more comfortable fit.

Instead of a wedding gown, you may choose a tailored white or pastel suit, or a flowing dress in a floral fabric. It can be any length you like, and any color that flatters you. Instead of the veil you wore the first time, wear a picture hat or flowers in your hair.

If you are planning to wear your wedding gown, your husband may wear a tuxedo. Otherwise, a suit is fine. The tie should be a special favorite, perhaps a gift from you!

If this is to be a formal ceremony with bridesmaids, ushers, a maid of honor, and a best man, the wedding party must not be more formally dressed than the bride and groom. They are not expected to match, as younger bridesmaids do.

The Ceremony

The reaffirmation ceremony can take place in a church with a reception following, or at the same location as the reception. Perhaps you'll have the ceremony in the church in which you were married.

Travel to the church by limousine, horse and buggy, or any way you wish. Your children can accompany you. For a special touch, rent a car that was made the year you were married. Vintage automobile clubs in your area will be able to help you with this.

Use ushers if there are over twenty-five guests. If only a handful of guests will be present, they can gather around you and your husband as you say your vows.

For an informal renewal of wedding vows there is no processional. You and your husband join the clergy in front of the assembled guests. At a church service, most couples prefer a processional. If your attendants are husband and wife, they should walk together. Your children should also be included in the processional. Depending on their ages, you may have them as attendants.

Although the husband and wife usually walk up the aisle together, your husband can also wait for you at the altar (as he did the first time). In that case, you will walk up the aisle alone, with your children, or even escorted by your father!

In a church, the wedding music will be played on an organ. At home, recorded music or a keyboard will be a likely choice. If you have rented a venue, find out if they have a grand piano, or hire a string trio or quartet. For the processional and the recessional, play the music you had for your first wedding, or a piece that has a sentimental meaning to you.

Vows

Many couples adapt their original wedding vows; others write new ones. Some combine both options. Do whichever makes the ceremony most meaningful for you.

Since you may be every bit as nervous as you were the first time, give your officiant a copy of the vows you have written. If you forget what to say, he can prompt you.

Be sure the content of your vows is appropriate. It's always nice to include references to your children and your life together. If you have had problems in the past, or have reconciled after a separation, a vague reference to love conquering all will suffice; it is not necessary to reveal the details.

Some couples quote poetry. If you wish to include Scripture, I recommend the following:

- Proverbs 31:10-13
- Hosea 2:21-22
- Ruth 1:6
- Genesis 2:18-24
- Song of Solomon 4:1-3
- Song of Solomon 5:10-14
- Isaiah 61:10
- Isaiah 62:5
- Hebrews 13:4
- Ecclesiastes 4:9-12

I have adapted the traditional wedding service to accommodate reaffirmation for the Catholic, Jewish, and Protestant faiths, and an interdenominational service. Use these, or change them to fit your needs.

Catholic

If this rite is to take place within a Eucharistic liturgy, it will come after the homily and Scripture readings. It can also stand alone. Choose meaningful Scripture readings, perhaps one of the following:

- Matthew 5:1-12, 13-16
- Matthew 22:35-40
- Genesis 2:18-24
- 1 Corinthians 13:4-7
- Ephesians 5:25-32
- Romans 8:31-39
- Romans 12:1-2

The Ritual: Begin with a hymn. After greeting those in attendance, the priest will open with a prayer. All will sit for Scripture readings and homily, after which you and your husband will come forward.

Rite of Reconciliation: Priest: God's word testifies to his abiding love for us; despite our faults he is always ready to forgive. Inspired and strengthened by His love, let us forgive one another from our hearts.

Husband: (Wife's Name), I ask forgiveness from God, from you, and from our family for all my faults and shortcomings, and with God's help I will try to grow in love.

Wife: (Husband's Name), I ask forgiveness from God, from you, and from our family for all my faults and shortcomings, and with God's help I will try to grow in love.

Priest: May God in His mercy forgive all our sins and bring us to everlasting life. All: Amen.

Rite of Reaffirmation: Priest: And now, before God and in the presence of your family and friends, I invite you to renew your marriage vows.

Husband: I, (Name), reaffirm my marriage vows to you, (Name). I promise to be true to you for better or worse, for richer or poorer, in sickness and in health, until death.

Wife: I, (Name), reaffirm my marriage vows to you, (Name). I promise to be true to you for better or worse, for richer or poorer, in sickness and in health, until death.

Priest: Gracious Father, bless this couple who have come before You with generous and grateful hearts. Fill them with Your Spirit that they may continue to be signs of Your abiding love and fidelity. We ask this in the name of Jesus, our Lord.

All: Amen.

Priest: You may kiss your bride.

If there is to be a Eucharist you will return to your seats. The General Intercessions follow, and the priest will prepare the Gifts. Otherwise, the priest will bless you and a concluding hymn will be sung. For General Intercessions, it is appropriate to have guests and family make petitions to express their hopes for your marriage, and to ask for God's blessings.

Jewish

Welcome: Rabbi: In every successful marriage there are not two partners, but three: man, woman, and God. "Shalom" is a state of wholeness and peace. All human beings are created in God's image. As it says in the Scripture, "When God created man, He made him in His likeness; male and female He created them." We are here today for a solemn but joyful reason. We are to witness the reaffirmation of the wedding vows that (Name) and (Name) made to each other on their wedding day, (date).

Vows: Husband: I have betrothed thee to me forever. I have betrothed thee in loving kindness and compassion.

Wife: I belong to my beloved as he belongs to me. When I found him whom my soul loveth, I held him and would not let him go. Set me as a seal unto thy heart, as a sign upon thine arm, for love is as strong as death. Many waters cannot quench love, neither can floods drown it.

Rabbi: The Rabbi who officiated at your wedding reminded you that since the Babylon exile in the year 586 Before the Common Era, Jews have always vowed to recall Jerusalem above their greatest joys. Today, as you reaffirm your marriage vows, you also reaffirm your loyalty to Jewish people the world over, to our religious heritage, and to your identification with our people's homeland in the land of Israel.

Reading: The Rabbi may choose a reading from the prophet Isaiah.

Prayers: Husband and wife: Blessed be thou, oh Lord our God, King of the universe, who has sustained us in life and has enabled us to reach the (anniversary, significant point) in our marriage.

All: Mazel Tov! Good luck and much happiness!

Protestant

The service may begin with a Scripture reading. You and your husband will stand at the altar during the reading, or the clergy may call you up afterward.

Welcome: Clergy: (Name) and (Name) are here today to thank God for His blessings during their (number) years of marriage. On their wedding day (date), they stood before God and promised to live together according to their sacred wedding vows. They have praised God for their blessings and depended upon Him when their lives were in trouble. They are joined here today by their children.

Prayer: The clergy will insert a prayer of his own, followed by The Lord's Prayer.

Blessing of the rings: The rings that have been worn during the past (number) years have been tested by fire, just as the Bible says gold must be tested. (Name) and (Name) have come through the fire as precious in God's sight as the gold in these rings. We thank God for His grace and mercy.

Vows: Husband: (Name), you are God's gift to me. Like this ring, our love will never be broken. I will continue to love you as Christ loves His church, until we are separated by death.

Wife: (Name), you are God's gift to me. Like this ring, our love will never be broken. I will continue to love you as Christ loves His church, until we are separated by death.

Clergy: You may kiss your bride.

The service concludes with a hymn, followed by the benediction.

Interdenominational

Opening: The service will open with a short Scriptural passage, perhaps Genesis 2:18. Clergy: The quality of love is that which gives meaning to all human relations. Traditionally, the relationship of love in a marriage between a man and a woman is the most profound of all. On this occasion, we are witnessing the affirmation of those vows of love made between (Name) and (Name) on their wedding day, (date).

Vows: Clergy: (Name and Name), we are gathered here today to witness the confirmation of your undying love for each other.

Husband: I, (Name), will continue to love and respect you, (Name), as my wife, for better or worse, for richer or poorer, in sickness and in health, for as long as we both shall live.

Wife: I, (Name), will continue to love and respect you, (Name), as my husband, for better or worse, for richer or poorer, in sickness and in health, for as long as we both shall live.

Candle-lighting: The family can light a candle from a cluster, or you and your husband can do this alone. "Our love is like a candle that we hold. Storms and winds can extinguish the flame, but our love gives us protection against the storm. In the light and the warmth of the candle, we see a symbol of the warm and illuminating love we share. We now light one candle from two, one life from two."

Declaration: Clergy: Since you have spoken your affirmation vows before God and your friends and family, our prayers are for your long and happy life together. God bless you. You may kiss your bride.

The Reception

Your reception celebration can take place anywhere a wedding reception is held: a hotel, a banquet hall, or your home. For a smaller group, you might plan dinner at a restaurant.

For more than twenty guests, or for a sit-down dinner, hire a caterer. Many couples handle smaller celebrations themselves, with help from friends and family.

As with any wedding, the wedding cake is a part of the festivities. The throwing of the bouquet and garter are out of place here, though.

The occasion definitely calls for a toast. Your son or the original best man will most likely do the honors.

Use the information in Chapter 13 when hiring vendors and planning the various aspects of the reception. When working with your photographer, don't overlook this opportunity for a family portrait.

Recorded dance music is often the choice at a home reception, but for larger affairs a DJ or band can be hired. Choose "your song" for the first dance. This may be a song you danced to at your wedding, or one that implies a long-lasting relationship, such as:

- *The Story of My Life*, by Neil Diamond
- *You're Still the One*, by Shania Twain
- *The Way We Were*, by Barbra Streisand
- *Are You Still in Love With Me*? by Anne Murray

A Second Honeymoon

There is no better way to end a reaffirmation than a second honeymoon (or perhaps a first!)

You may wish to return to the location of your first honeymoon. Or, perhaps you've always wanted to take a cruise. Your travel agent has ideas and brochures to help you decide. After twenty-five years together, you will have different interests than a newlywed couple.

Reaffirmation Day Timeline

The night before:

Have a rehearsal; be sure everyone knows where to stand at the altar and the order in which to walk down the aisle (if you are having a processional.) See Chapter 10 for more information on rehearsals.

The morning:

Go over your checklists with the caterers; decorate the hall, home, or church; make sure the cake and floral delivery is as scheduled.

2 hours before:

Get dressed.

30 minutes before:

If you will be having ushers, they will begin seating the guests.

15 minutes before:

Arrive at the church with your husband and children; the wedding party arrives. If the reaffirmation will be at your home, the clergy will arrive at this time.

5 minutes before:

All guests are seated; the prelude music plays. The ceremony begins.

For Your Notes

CHAPTER 22

Planning the Honeymoon

The Choices are Endless

Early in your planning stages, decide where to go for your honeymoon and begin to put your plans into action.

Call your travel agent or go online. Book early to avoid disappointment. Be sure to investigate thoroughly. Consider such things as inoculations and travel advisories. When is hurricane season? Is it unbearably hot during the summer months?

A growing number of couples are opting to take shorter local trips. Many check into a hotel right in their own city.

Honeymoon at Home

Some newlyweds would rather spend their money on something else. They honeymoon right in their own home! They aren't missing a thing! If this sounds good to you, here are a few ideas:

- Hire a cleaning lady beforehand, so there is nothing for you to do
- Light the fireplace
- Have fresh flowers *everywhere*
- Take the phone off the hook
- Indulge in a luxurious bubble bath
- Have a picnic on the living room floor

- Dress up and have a movie night with videos
- Go out and act like tourists
- Have a midnight snack that includes champagne

Honeymoon Planning Checklist

DESTINATION

DURATION OF HONEYMOON

WEDDING NIGHT

Hotel
Address
Telephone
Email
Fax
Reservation number
Confirmed
Rate
Notes:

TRAVEL AGENT

Agency
Agent
Address
Telephone
E-mail
Fax
Notes:

TRAVEL PLANS:

Departure date
Time
Flight number
Airline
Arrival date
Time
Departure date

Time
Flight number
Airline
Arrival date
Time

HOTEL(S):

Hotel
Address
Telephone
Email
Fax
Arrival date
Departure date
Confirmed

Hotel
Address
Telephone
Email
Arrival Date
Departure Date
Confirmed

INSURANCE: BRIDE

Name of company
Policy number

INSURANCE: GROOM

Name of company
Policy number

IMMUNIZATIONS: BRIDE

Type
Date

Type
Date
Type
Date

IMMUNIZATIONS: GROOM

Type
Date
Type
Date
Type
Date

PASSPORT: BRIDE

Date applied for
Received

PASSPORT: GROOM

Date applied for
Received

RENTAL CAR:

Name of company
Telephone
E-mail
Fax
Type of car
Pick-up
Drop off
Rate
Insurance
International driver's license

Honeymoon Packing Checklist

- Driver's license
- Marriage license/certificate
- Passports
- Proof of inoculations
- Visas
- Airline tickets
- Birth certificates
- Traveler's checks
- List of important telephone numbers
- Reading glasses
- Sun glasses
- Camera, video
- Battery charger
- Aspirin, Tylenol
- Toothbrush, toothpaste, mouthwash
- Deodorant
- Prescriptions
- Hair dyer, curling iron
- Voltage convertor
- Razor, blades
- Brush, comb
- Hairspray, mousse
- Band-Aids
- Perfume, aftershave
- Hand lotion
- Underwear
- Bathing suit
- Casual clothes
- Dress clothes
- Sweater, jacket
- Shoes, sandals
- Robes
- Other

For Your Notes

CHAPTER

23

Setting Up Your New Home

Room-by-Room

Whether you are setting up your first home, getting married for a second time, or have been living together for some time, you will be incorporating your new wedding gifts into your home.

Before going to the gift registry, sit down together and think of everything you want to have in your home. The following lists should help.

The Kitchen

Do you like to cook? What kind of cooking? Do you bake often, or just at Christmas? Use the following list, as well as the lists of pots and pans, electrical appliances, and informal dining in this chapter to determine your kitchen needs.

Kitchen knives:

- Paring knife
- Chef's knife
- Bread knife
- Steak knives
- Carving set
- Grapefruit knife

Kitchen linens:

- Tea towels
- Oven mitts
- Aprons
- Pot holders

Kitchen basics:

- Measuring cups
- Measuring spoons
- Mixing bowls
- Utensil set
- Canisters
- Other (specify)

The Dining Room:

Using the sections on linens, flatware, glassware, and dinnerware in this chapter to determine your dining room needs.

The Bedroom:

Use the following, plus the section on linens in this chapter, to determine your bedroom needs.

- Clock radio
- Telephone
- Television
- Breakfast trays
- Closet organizers
- Other: (specify)

The Bathroom:

Use the following, plus the section on linen in this chapter, to determine your bathroom needs.

- Shower curtain/liner
- Soap dish/lotion dispenser/tissue box cover/shower curtain hooks/ waste basket
- Scale
- Bath mat
- Magnifying mirror
- Other (specify)

The Living Room:

Many of these items can also be used in other rooms:

- Vases
- Candleholders
- Lamps
- Picture frames
- Framed prints
- Sculptures
- Wine rack
- Fireplace tools
- Television
- Electronics

Linens

The word "linen" is commonly used for household textiles, such as sheets, tablecloths, and towels. Real linen is made of flax. It is expensive but exquisite.

Traditional tablecloths are commonly made of damask. It is woven in a tone-on-tone pattern that features matte and lustrous areas. Matching napkins are a must. As well as linen, damask is made of cotton, polyester, and blends. Lace tablecloths are lovely alone or over a colored tablecloth.

Know the measurements of your table before shopping or registering for tablecloths. Allow an overhang of eighteen inches or forty-five centimeters. Shop or register for the kitchen as well as for the dining room.

Protector pads are necessary for all tables. They save wooden tables from heat damage, but they are also recommended for glass tables. They muffle the sounds of objects coming in contact with the table, and pad the surface so that a crystal wine glass that is knocked over won't break.

Moving to the bedroom, sheets and pillowcases are available in different thread counts. The highest is 310 threads per square inch, with 180 earning the name percale. Cotton is the most comfortable and is longwearing. Start with three sets of sheets and pillowcases.

Pillows are available in standard and queen sizes. They can be filled with down, feathers, fiberfill, or foam. Prices vary.

Other bedroom linens include comforters, pillow shams, duvets, duvet covers, mattress pads, and dust ruffles.

Bath towels, hand towels, and face cloths are available in different thicknesses. The thicker they are, the more expensive. Some have big terry loops; others are sheared on one side to create a velvety texture. Bath sheets are extra large towels that are very luxurious. A set of six of each size makes a good start.

Table Linens:

- Formal tablecloth and napkins
- Informal tablecloth and napkins
- Placemats and napkins
- Table protector pad
- Runner

Bedroom Linens:

- Flat top sheets
- Fitted bottom sheets
- Pillowcases
- Blanket(s)
- Comforter
- Duvet
- Duvet cover
- Pillow shams
- Dust ruffle

Bathroom Linens:

- Bath towels
- Bath sheets
- Hand towels
- Face cloths

Choosing Flatware

Flatware is available in stainless steel for casual dining, and sterling or silver-plate for more formal occasions. Choose a service for eight, ten, or twelve, depending on your entertaining needs.

Stainless steel is usually made of eighteen percent chromium and eight percent nickel. This is indicated by the numerals 18/8. Nickel is what gives stainless steel its luster; the more expensive and lustrous stainless is 18/10. Many stainless patterns are similar to those of sterling, making it possible for couples on a budget to create formal looks. Stainless is easy to care for and will last for years.

Sterling is 92.5 percent silver with small amounts of other metals, such as copper. It is the most expensive flatware. Sterling is heavier than other flatware, and is identified by a hallmark stamped on the back.

Silver-plate is pure silver that has been electroplated onto an item of nickel, copper, or zinc. It looks much like sterling, but is less expensive. The amount of silver used in plating will determine the quality. Many patterns have gold-plated accents.

Both sterling and silver-plate must be polished to remove tarnish. Storing in a specially-treated cloth bag or cutlery chest will cut down drastically on the amount of polishing that will need to be done. Both will accumulate a network of fine scratches as they are used. These will eventually form the "patina" of the piece, making it even more valuable. Never store silver in plastic, put it in the dishwasher, or let it come in contact with rubber bands.

Choose your flatware set from among these many pieces:

- Salad fork: A small fork that can be also used for cake and other desserts
- Dinner fork: A standard-sized fork, used for the entrée

- Seafood or cocktail fork: A fork which has very short tines and a long handle
- Dinner knife: A standard-sized knife
- Butter spreader: Used for buttering rolls, placed on the bread and butter plate
- Teaspoon: A standard-sized spoon
- Small teaspoon: Smaller than a teaspoon, sometimes called a demitasse spoon
- Tablespoon: Larger than a teaspoon
- Coffee spoon: The smallest spoon
- Soup spoon: A large spoon with a rounded bowl
- Iced tea spoon: Teaspoon-sized, but with a long handle
- Grapefruit spoon: Teaspoon-sized, but with serrated section at the tip
- Sugar spoon: Often shell-shaped, placed in the sugar bowl
- Butter knife: A small knife, placed on the butter dish
- Casserole spoon: A very large spoon, used for serving
- Serving spoon: Smaller than a casserole spoon, available plain and slotted
- Ladle: A round bowl with the handle set at an angle. Soup ladles are large, gravy ladles are much smaller
- Meat fork: A very large fork, used for cold cuts
- Salad servers: A set consisting of a long-handled spoon and fork
- Carving set: A very sharp knife and long-tined fork, used for carving meat
- Cake server: Trowel-shaped for lifting cakes, pies, and other desserts

Holloware

Serving pieces that are made of silver, china, crystal, or glass are commonly called hollowware. If you are choosing hollowware in china, you can match or contrast with your pattern. Purchase or register for these hollowware pieces:

- Salt and pepper shakers
- Serving trays

- Platters
- Teapot
- Coffee pot
- Cream and sugar
- Wine cooler
- Ice bucket and tongs
- Vegetable dishes
- Gravy boat
- Cake plate

Dinnerware

Fine china may appear fragile, but it is actually very strong. It is made of refined clays and powdered minerals, and is fired for long periods of time. A variation is bone china, to which bone ash is added. It is fired at a lower temperature, and has a white, translucent appearance. When china is chipped, it will not absorb grease or discolor. Both types are resistant to crazing (the fine cracks that cover some older pieces) and will ring when tapped. Often, a gold rim is used as an accent.

Porcelain is first fired at a low temperature, then the glaze is applied and the piece is fired at a very high temperature.

Ironstone is made of ball clay and feldspar. It often has a relief pattern. It is sturdy and a good choice for everyday use.

Stoneware is a ceramic, made of clay mixed with feldspar, quartz, kaolin, and aluminum oxide. It is fired at very high temperatures and has a neutral glaze finish.

Depending on your entertainment needs, you will probably want to register for two sets, one for everyday dining and the other for formal occasions. Informal dinnerware is sold in sets of four place settings; expensive china patterns are sold by the piece or open stock.

Charger plates are not meant to come in contact with food, but provide a surface upon which to place the dinner plate. They are usually metal or plastic with a metallic finish.

Choose from these pieces:

- Dinner plate
- Salad plate

- Bread and butter plate
- Soup bowl
- Cream soup (two handles and a separate saucer)
- Cereal bowl
- Dessert bowl
- Cup and saucer
- Coffee mug
- Charger plate

Glassware and Crystal

Glass and crystal can often be used interchangeably, although crystal is more formal. Stronger than is commonly thought, crystal is made by adding lead to the glass. A lead content of 24 percent earns it the right to be called "lead crystal."

The best quality pieces have a clear, lustrous appearance. Inferior pieces will have a slight tint. Cut glass and crystal are especially beautiful by candlelight, and the clearest glass will give the best effect. Also look for smooth rims. Bubbles and other imperfections are the sign of a handmade item, and are not considered flaws.

A distinguishing feature of crystal is the ring you hear when the glass is tapped. It is affected by the thickness, shape, and size of the glass, and therefore should not be used as an indication of quality.

Do not try to collect glasses in every size; many can do double duty. For the average household, a set of five glasses will serve you well: tall glasses (highballs), short glasses (old-fashioned), wine glasses, champagne flutes, and water goblets. Six or eight in each size should be plenty. Choose from the following sizes of glasses:

- White wine
- Red wine
- Water goblet
- Champagne flute
- Sherbet
- Liqueur
- Sherry
- Brandy

- Juice
- Pilsner
- Beer mug
- Old-fashioned
- Highball

Add to this:

- Coasters
- Ashtrays
- Juice/water pitcher

Electrical Appliances

Shop around and compare features. Buy only the electrical appliances you have room to store and those you will actually use. The choices are many:

- Grill
- Can opener
- Blender
- Hand mixer
- Coffee maker
- Espresso maker
- Cappuccino maker
- Wok
- Crock or slow cooker
- Toaster
- Food processor
- Bread maker
- Juicer
- Ice cream or yogurt maker
- Kettle
- Toaster oven
- Microwave

Pots and Pans

Pots and pans are sold open stock (separately) or in boxed sets. Open stock means that each pot will have its own lid. When purchased as a set, frying pans are designed to share a lid with one of the pots. But remember, you can only cook with four pots at a time!

Just about any kitchen can operate nicely with the following:

- 3 saucepans: small, medium, large
- 1 frying pan
- 1 Dutch oven
- 1 large stock pot
- 1 double boiler
- 1 roasting pan (with rack)
- 2 pie pans
- 2 round cake pans
- 1 cookie sheet
- 2 square pans
- 1 loaf pan
- 1 muffin pan

If you do much baking you may want to increase these numbers. Serious cooks might add items such as these:

- Wok
- Pasta cooker
- Steamer
- Omelet pan
- Poacher

There is a wide choice of materials, including those with non-stick interiors. Some of these are:

- Stainless steel, with or without a copper bottom
- Copper
- Cast iron
- Cast iron coated with porcelain

- Anodized aluminum
- Aluminum coated with stainless steel

Many cooks choose the material to match the purpose, rather than opting for a matched set. Register for quality pots and pans that will last a lifetime. They should be heavy enough for strength, but not so heavy as to be difficult to lift when full. Thick walls and bottoms will cook better. The bottoms must be completely flat for even heat distribution.

Consider your storage space. If the pots and pans have holes in the handles, register for a pot rack to save cupboard space.

Monograms

There are five different monogram options, all of which are equally acceptable, although not for use in all situations. If Laura Michelle Aldridge marries William David Taunton, the options will be as follows:

- The bride's married initials (LT)
- The bride's maiden initials on either side of the groom's initial (LTA)
- The couple's married surname only (T)
- The surname initials of the bride and groom (TA)
- The first initials of the bride and groom on either side of their surname (LTW) For the groom's personal items, his surname (T) or both initials (WT) are correct.

Monograms can be very simple, or quite ornate. A silver tray will look better with an elaborate monogram, and a bath towel with a simpler one. "Less is more" applies here.

Silver flatware can be monogrammed so that the initials can be read by the person seated at the table, or so that they can be read while holding the piece. If you collect heirloom silver, it is possible to have your initials added to the ones already there.

Silver hollowware can also be monogrammed, and trays often feature a smooth surface in the center for this purpose.

Napkins are monogrammed diagonally on one corner. If a tablecloth is monogrammed, the monogram must fall between the edge of the table and the hem, never on the table surface. Towels are monogrammed in the center of one end. Pillowcases are done with the monogram in the center of the open end. The monogram on a top sheet is inside the top hem, at the center. That way, it will be seen when the sheet is turned down.

For Your Notes

Conclusion

And now you will take what you have learned in these pages and plan the wedding of your dreams. I wish you both luck, love, and a lifetime of happiness together!

As you and your new groom settle happily into married life, you will find yourself wishing you could do it all again. You miss the excitement you felt when planning your wedding. You loved every minute of it, and you're sorry it's all over so soon.

Why not consider becoming a professional wedding planner? Turn your newfound wedding-planning skills into a business! You certainly have experience; now get the training!

The Sandcastles Wedding Consultant Certification Programme combines the convenience of a home-study format with the affordability of a pay-as-you-go plan.

The course is divided into 14 modules, plus the final exam. There are two textbooks. The first is this book, *Weddingology*, which is used to teach the student how to plan weddings. The second, *The Sandcastles Guide to Starting and Managing Your Own Wedding-Planning Business*, tells you all you need to know about the business end of the profession.

For more information, or to get started, go to my Web site,

http://www.sharigrenier.com

Printed in the United States
By Bookmasters